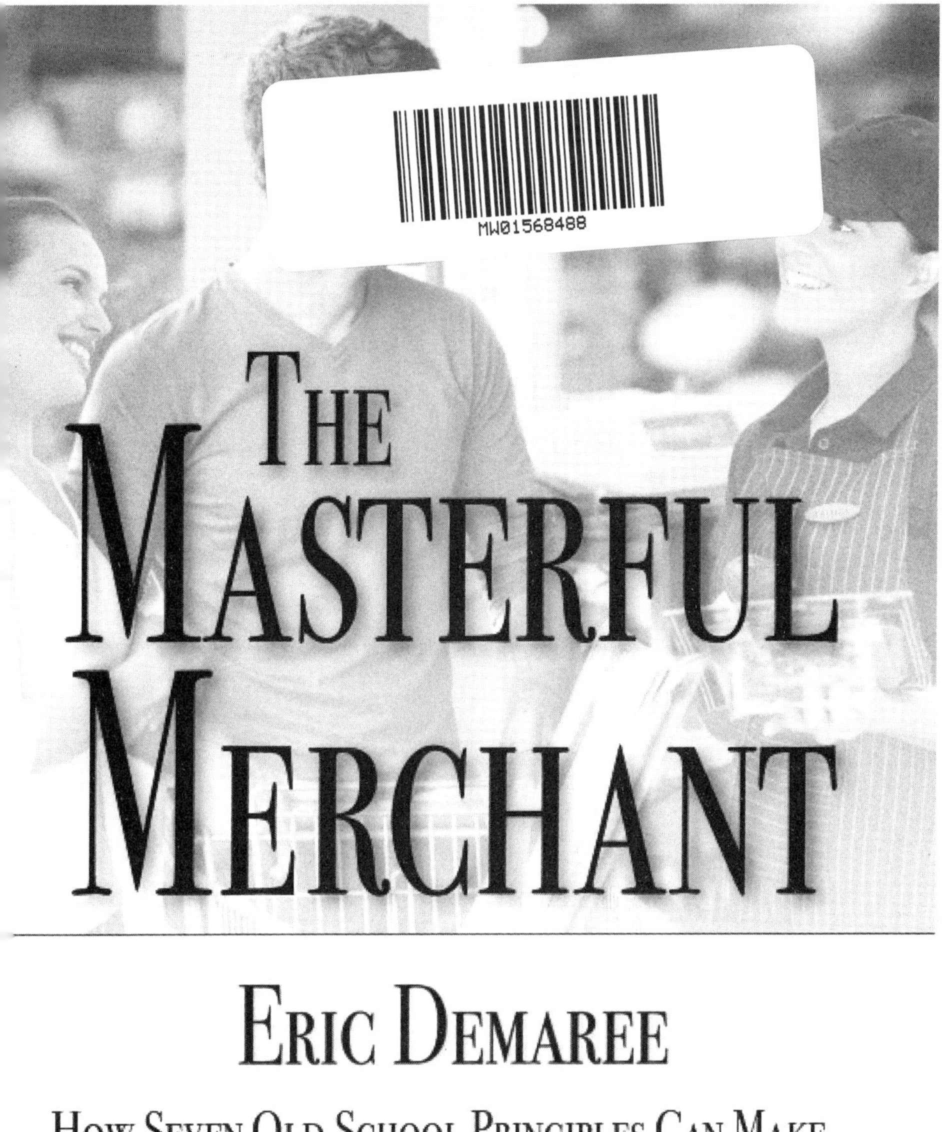

THE MASTERFUL MERCHANT

Eric Demaree

How Seven Old School Principles Can Make Modern Day Retailers More Successful

FOREWORD BY

Robert A. Rohm, Ph.D.

THE MASTERFUL MERCHANT

How Seven Old School Principles Can Make Modern Day Retailers More Successful

Eric Demaree

Personality
INSIGHTS
PRESS

© Copyright 2016 Eric Demaree
Part Three © 2016 Personality Insights Inc.
Dr. Robert A. Rohm
All Rights Reserved

Editor – April Dawn
Graphic design – Pedro A. Gonzalez

No part of this book may be reproduced or transmitted in any form or by any means, including photocopying, without permission in writing from the publisher.

Published by Personality Insights, Inc.
P.O. Box 28592 • Atlanta, GA 30358-0592
1.800.509.DISC • www.personalityinsights.com

ISBN: 978-0-9836898-8-1

Printed in the United States of America

Table of Contents

7
Dedication

9
Acknowledgments

11
Foreword

13
Introduction

19
PART ONE - THE FABLE

21
CHAPTER ONE - Potholes

33
CHAPTER TWO - Discovering the First Principle

41
CHAPTER THREE - Building a G.O.R. Culture

47
CHAPTER FOUR - The Second and Third Principles Revealed

53
CHAPTER FIVE - The Ultimate Promoter

57
CHAPTER SIX - The Simplicity of Best - Better - Good

61
CHAPTER SEVEN - A Broken Promise

Table of Contents *continued*

65 CHAPTER EIGHT - The Seventh Principle Revealed
73 CHAPTER NINE - Two Years Later
77 CHAPTER TEN - The Lessons
81 **PART TWO** WORLD-CLASS COMPANIES ARE BEATING THEIR COMPETITION THROUGH A CUSTOMER FIRST CULTURE
85 **PRINCIPLE No. 1** People – The Right People
109 **PART THREE** UNDERSTANDING THE MODEL OF HUMAN BEHAVIOR By Robert A. Rohm, Ph.D.
111 People 101
113 Understanding Human Behavior
155 Building Rapport
187 About the Author

To my Carpet One Floor & Home family, the most spirited, hardworking, entrepreneurial group of retailers who understand the value of putting people first

Acknowledgements

First, I thank my wife, Lynne, for your love and forgiveness and for the sacrifices you have made to support me and our family. You have blessed me over the past 41 years with your guidance and patience. *Thank you, sweetheart, for hanging in there.*

For all the friends, family and business professionals who have helped me along the way, thank you. I especially want to thank the founders of CCA Global Partners, Alan Greenberg and Howard Brodsky, for their business acumen, their passion and their entrepreneurial spirit.

Thank you, Pat Farrah. I wore out a lot of shoes walking stores with you. I will be forever grateful for the tough lessons you shared with me.

Thank you, Dr. Robert Rohm and your team at Personality Insights Inc. You gave me the courage to take a simple story and publish it. You helped me in more ways than I can ever say. *God Bless you.*

Thank you, Lord. Thank you for providing me the opportunity to meet so many wonderful and amazing people.

Foreword

I remember a few years ago the first time I met Eric Demaree. He instantly struck me as one of those rare individuals you meet for the first time who is "bigger than life". These kind of people immediately strike you as energetic individuals who can walk right up to you and greet you with confidence and a big smile.

My mind has different categories inside of it to help me relate successfully to the people I meet. I can still remember the first time I met many other notable leaders. There is just something about these kind of people that is dynamic and different. They have a sense of destiny and confidence about them – like they know where they are headed and they want to take you with them! I immediately put Eric Demaree in that category!

The book you are about to read is a parable or a story that is used to teach an important truth. The word "parable" comes from two Greek words: "para" which means "along-side" (from which we get the English word parallel) and the word "bola" which means "to throw" (from which we get the English word bowling). Thus, a parable is a story that is thrown out along side of a teaching in order to help illustrate or explain an important truth. You are going to enjoy this experience. You are going to learn some familiar truths in a brand new way! You will also remember this story for days to come!

Don't be surprised if you find yourself remembering this story as you work with your clients and customers in the coming days! It is simple enough to understand and practical enough to apply! I love this kind of learning. As a former educator for over forty years, I believe it is the best way to learn!

Thank you Eric Demaree for taking the time, effort and energy to complete this work. You now rank in the small, rare group of the people in the world who are authors. Your creativity is excellent, and your ability to communicate an old truth in a new and fresh way is so enjoyable! Your years in retail sales have given you understanding and insights that would take other people a lifetime to learn.

May you, the reader, benefit greatly from this excellent work!

Robert A. Rohm, Ph.D., President, CEO
Personality Insights, Inc.
Atlanta, GA

INTRODUCTION

"Your Experience is Going to Make You Fail!"

Those words came from Bernie Marcus, the founder of The Home Depot. They were directed right at me, a new product merchant and buyer on my very first store walk. There I stood, a former big shot executive, in a shiny new orange apron with my name carefully handwritten under the announcement, "HELLO, MY NAME IS...ERIC".

When Bernie walked a Home Depot store, he was always surrounded by a sea of "orange blooded" associates. They gazed at Bernie like he was a rock star. When he spoke, people hung on his every word. He worked the crowd like a seasoned politician with the timing of a standup comic. (I learned much later that after Bernie received his degree in pharmacy, he worked in the Catskills in upstate New York, an area well known for its comedians.)

Within the first few minutes of my inaugural walk, Mr. Marcus shouted, "WHERE'S THIS NEW FLOORING GUY? COME UP HERE!" Despite being 39 years old and having held executive level positions with several former companies, I sheepishly moved my way through the crowd like a scolded child until I stood face to face with Bernie.

Grabbing me by the arm, Bernie spun me around until I was facing a sea of orange aprons. Looking across a mass of smirking, laughing and smiling faces, Bernie hit me with the most powerful words I have ever heard...

"YOU KNOW, THE PROBLEM I HAVE WITH YOU IS, YOUR EXPERIENCE IS GOING TO MAKE YOU FAIL."

WOW! My first week and I'm already failing. My head spun with thoughts of "Oh my gosh - is my first walk going to be my last!?"

Thankfully, that store walk was the first of thousands of store walks I took as a Merchant and as a Vice President. Bernie's words were a wakeup call for me. He wanted to make the point that, to be successful, you cannot think you know it all. Despite your experience and your expertise, you have to get out into the real world and talk to customers and talk to store associates. You have to be open to every idea and be willing to take the best of what people tell you and effectively implement ideas that will benefit the customer.

Successful Merchants do not let their experience prevent them from asking frontline sales associates and customers how to do things better. Pat Farrah, the founding Merchant of The Home Depot, gave me some very sage advice, "Successful Merchants get out from behind their corporate desks and get into stores to find out what is happening in the real world. You can find all the answers you need in the aisles of our stores."

Over the course of my career, I have tried to stay true to that advice. I spent twelve years helping Depot build their business. I started as a product merchant for the floor, wall and organization department, working my way up to Vice President of Merchandising for the Home Depot stores and their Expo Design Center division. Through a lot of hard work and luck, I moved on to become President of Carpet One Floor & Home, a division of CCA Global Partners.

The Masterful Merchant

CCA is an international buying cooperative made up of thousands of independently owned and operated retailers. This amazing group of entrepreneurially spirited business people, along with my trial by fire experience with The Home Depot, motivated me to write this book.

Anyone who has worked in retail understands how important it is to keep pace with today's consumer. Technology has given all of us an endless sea of virtual stores that are open twenty-four hours a day, seven days each week. With one click, we have a world of products and options available to us. As consumers, we are in control of how we want to shop, when we want to shop and with whom we want to shop. Every day we are given more and more options to satisfy our appetites to buy.

Many retailers are struggling with this rapid change in consumer buying habits. They have hired legions of people to build sophisticated websites, CRM systems and automated digital marketing strategies executed through every electronic and social media platform imaginable. Technology, however, can be easily copied and as important as it is, it cannot, on its own, differentiate companies from one another.

The modern day retailers can only win by staffing their stores with caring people and training them to become Masterful Merchants. The best of the best have a culture where their people are empowered to take care of customers. People who are customer-centric and who want to take care of each other are the Masterful Merchants.

Bernie Marcus, Pat Farrah, and other great leaders, like Howard Brodsky and Alan Greenberg, the co-founders of CCA Global Partners, built great companies because they have within them a competitive fire. They have passion and compassion. They have a deep desire to help others, in business and in life. They built a caring culture within their companies. They understood that the best way to generate bottom line profits is through talented, loyal, and dedicated People.

PART 1 of The Masterful Merchant is written as a fable. It is a story based on many of the things I personally experienced over the course of my career. I have tried to capture some of the lessons that I have learned about retailing from many great teachers and from entrepreneurial store owners. There is nothing revolutionary within these pages. Any reference to people or places in the book is purely fictional, but there is one over-riding message that I hope everyone takes away from this story. That message is this...

EVERYTHING STARTS AND ENDS WITH PEOPLE!

When you have People who have a sense of humanity and humility, who have deep within them a willingness to take care of others, and who always try to do what is in the best interest of others, you will build a successful business.

In **PART 2** of the book, I give some suggestions on how to create a "**Customer First Culture**". In **PART 3**, Dr. Robert Rohm shares his valuable insights into understanding the **DISC Model of Human Behavior.** There are specific skills you can use to improve your understanding of what drives people and of how to best communicate with each personality type to build a better culture and a stronger team. If it is true that everything starts and ends with people, then understanding people becomes paramount in every interaction.

I hope somewhere within these pages you pick up a simple lesson or two. It was a joy writing this book and revisiting so many cherished (and some painful) memories. This is my tribute and thank you to all the many wonderful people who shared their wisdom and experience with me over the years.

I wish you all success in retailing and in your life.
Good luck and good selling! God bless you all.

Eric Demaree

PART ONE

THE FABLE

CHAPTER ONE

Potholes

"**Oh** shoot!" The words whistled across Bill's lips as he gingerly pulled his mud-soaked foot out of the gaping hole in the blacktop. How he managed to pull next to a pothole that would accommodate his size 13 shoes was a question that only briefly entered Bill's mind. Over the past ten years, Bill had stepped out onto the abandoned parking lots of hundreds of closed stores. In all that time, he could not remember ever having a personal encounter with a pothole, although he could not say the same for many of his rental cars.

Bill was usually very observant and aware of his surroundings, especially in his line of work. Commercial Retail Properties (CRP) relied on Bill Richardson to evaluate and assess buildings that were once thriving businesses and the pride of entrepreneurial business owners but were now hollow shells.

Most nights, when Bill climbed out of his car and stared at the front entrance of a dilapidated store, he wondered, "What happened? What caused this business to fail?" But tonight, his mud-caked shoe and his water-soaked sock occupied his only thoughts. He was hoping that somewhere inside the store he could find a place to clean up and dry off.

After a quick couple of shakes of his leg, Bill grabbed what looked like an Army duffle bag and walked toward the front door. The "beep-beep" of his door locks and the squishing of his left foot were the only sounds that disturbed the silence of the night. As he walked toward the front entrance, Bill pulled a pen light from his pocket, placed it between his teeth and, with a quick twist, pointed a beam of light at his tattered duffle bag.

The eerie pumpkin like glow emanating from his mouth provided enough light for Bill to see a large pile of dangling metal deep inside his bag. From the faint light reflecting off the shiny surfaces, you could tell there was an enormous ring lying on top of piles of assorted papers. It was bigger than a linebacker's thigh and held keys of every imaginable shape and size. Just looking at the countless number of keys made you wonder how Bill could find the right one that would open this particular building. But with the deft touch of a skilled magician, Bill flipped through the maze of clanging metal and pulled out the right key. He inserted it into the slot in the front door, but it didn't budge as he tried to turn the lock.

That came as no surprise to Bill. He expected a struggle. Old buildings that have been closed for some time always put up a fight whenever he had to jiggle their rusted locks. Turning the key with all his strength and bouncing off the door like a basketball, Bill drove his shoulder into the door over and over again until it begrudgingly moved. It opened just enough for him to squeeze through.

The musty smell that swirled inside the building was a familiar scent that Bill had experienced many times. There was also a hint of rotted produce in the air that served as a reminder that he had not looked at his paperwork to see what business used to occupy the cavernous space. With his trusty pen light still clenched between his teeth, Bill hoisted his duffle bag onto a dusty checkout counter.

His duffle bag was big enough to hold an assortment of tools necessary for evaluating any type of building. The green canvas fabric was torn and shredded and was held together by a long metal zipper that barely kept the secret contents of the bag from spilling out. Every

The Masterful Merchant

few inches, along the length of the zipper, there were missing teeth. It was a wonder how Bill ever got the bag to open, or once he did, how he ever closed it.

With a couple of grunts and groans, Bill wrestled the bag open and reached in to pull out an old-fashioned canister lantern. He set it on the counter and switched it on. The sudden brightness from the light caused him to quickly close his eyes. "Why do I do that every time?" Bill silently said to himself.

With his eyes still closed, he rummaged through his bag and pulled out a thick pile of papers. Wiping away the tears caused by the sting from the bright flash of light, Bill slowly opened his eyes, looked down at his paperwork, and read the words "O'Brien's Basket." "Hmmm," thought Bill, "must have been an old grocery store."

Holding up the lantern, he narrowed his eyes in an attempt to see better across the expanse of the building. In front of him were a row of cash registers standing like old soldiers in a perfectly straight line but looking like they had lost the battle. Faded register tapes lay in piles on the dust-covered checkout stand and the broken tiles scattered over the stained concrete floors were a grim reminder of a broken business.

"Definitely an old grocery store," Bill said out loud. He always wondered how many years loyal feet stood at registers like these, taking care of customers.

Turning toward the front of the store, Bill's thoughts were interrupted again by the squish squash of his left foot. As he bent down intending to take off his shoe and relieve his wrinkled toes from their watery tomb, he noticed a broken picture frame surrounding an old black and white photograph of people dressed in white aprons. Each person had their name embroidered on their apron directly above a wicker basket logo. Picking up the frame to get a closer look, Bill rubbed his thumb across the dusty plaque at the base of the photo. He could barely make out the inscription. It said: "O'Brien's

Basket. Our Customers Bring Out the Best in Us!" The big gleaming smiles on everyone's face assured Bill that he could believe every word he read.

The wrinkled photo brought a flood of memories back to Bill about his first job as a stock boy at Old Orchard. He smiled as his thoughts drifted back to his childhood and he thought about that great old place with all its exciting sights, sounds and smells. He imagined that O'Brien's Basket was a lot like Old Orchard, a neighborhood place where customers gathered to buy product from local vendors...as neighbors supporting neighbors.

Old Orchard was a destination for people all over New Jersey looking for the best in fresh fruit and baked goods. Its centerpiece was a red clapboard building that stood proudly against the backdrop of hundreds of apple trees. The anticipation of getting a fresh apple cinnamon donut after Sunday church service created excitement in many young children, as well as many moms and dads.

The minute you drove up the cobblestone driveway, you knew that Old Orchard was a special place. Smiling customers stood shoulder to shoulder along an endless row of white post-rail fence, just waiting for the opportunity to feed crisp apples to chestnut brown horses. Blue vested employees gave you a friendly wave as you circled in your car searching for a place to park.

The best part was when you were greeted at the front door. Every customer was always offered a small sample of that day's special. Whether it was a buttery, sweet almond cookie, a sip of cider, or a tart chunk of apple pie, that first taste upon entering the store was worth ten trips around the parking lot. One little bite, one little sip, was just the start of an exciting journey that waited for every customer within the four walls of the store. Old Orchard had so much character.

The interior was a visual feast. The walls were covered by wide wooden planks, the kind you would expect to see in an old barn. Stalks of corn rose out of the produce department like green sentries

The Masterful Merchant

guarding freshly picked, golden yellow ears. Apples spilled over wooden baskets in a cascade of green and red. Next to each produce station was a picture of a local farmer with a delightful homespun story about the product and the people. Old Orchard wanted customers to know the people in the community who grew such magnificent produce. What great local flavor!

In the back of the store were aisles and aisles of fresh baked pies and breads. It was impossible not to buy something when you walked by, especially when blue vested employees were always offering up free samples of pumpkin, cherry, apple, pecan pies and more. Almonds, walnuts, peanuts and mounds of cashews were just waiting to be scooped up into old fashion paper sacks. What a feast for the senses.

All over the store, little paper cups of apple cider sat on trays draped with red-and-white-checkered tablecloths. Each tray had a simple sign with a simple message, "Enjoy!" On one far wall were large oak wine barrels surrounded by wooden chairs, set up where people could play checkers while they listened to soft music and savored each sip of warm cider, fresh coffee or hot tea.

Old Orchard. "Ah, what great memories," Bill thought as he gazed at the photo of O'Brien's Basket. He knew from the faded photograph that the place where he was standing must have meant the world to the folks in this neighborhood. He knew that it once meant a lot to all the employees and customers who shopped there, just as much as Old Orchard had meant to him. "Memories of great places always fill your senses," Bill was fond of saying.

Setting down the photo, Bill glanced up at the hazy front windows where the name O'Brien's Basket was stenciled. The faded white and green lettering was cracked and peeling. It looked like someone had hand drawn the wicker basket logo under the store name. Along the front of each window, he could see the remnants of old signs promoting homegrown produce from neighborhood farms. He could also see a poster announcing "The King and I" at the local high school. It was propped up next to the free magazine stand. There was a copy of the 'local happenings' paper sitting alone on an old wooden stool. Bill smiled as he ran his hand over the dusty seat, remembering how he would have to 'occasionally' sit on such a stool in the corner of his grammar school classroom.

Blocking the front door and impeding Bill's entrance into the store were rows of shopping carts. Most were covered with rust and had wheels that wobbled when pushed or would not move at all. Some had little plaques that held advertisements, offering services like painting or a free oil filter with every Quaker State oil change from Joe's Garage (every town had a Joe's Garage).

Squish! Again with every step, Bill's little pothole incident reminded him that he needed to look for the restrooms. He held onto a faint hope that once he found one, there would be a towel to dry off his shoe and sock. So off he went, deeper into the store.

Walking past the first row of shelves, Bill noticed that the center of the store had very low racks of shelving. There was only high metal racking around the outside perimeter of this store. You could literally see across the majority of the store from front to back.

Reaching deep inside his duffle, Bill pulled out what looked like a police search light. As he switched it on, a powerful beam shot across the store and revealed large, poster-sized photos. One photo was a picture of kids eating watermelon at a picnic, and, despite the obvious effects of time, you could still see the juicy streams of melon streaking down every smiling face. In another, two kids were playfully spitting seeds at each other.

Another photo showed loving grandparents bending down to share some chocolate with their grandchildren. Being a grandfather, Bill was instantly captured by the moment. It was easy to put himself in the picture. His eyes twinkled as much as the man's in the photograph, especially when he thought about his own family. "Pops" was his favorite word and hearing it come out of his grandchildren's mouths was his favorite sound.

Walking toward the last photo at the farthest end of the store, Bill looked overhead and saw a slightly tilted sign that said RESTROOMS. Stepping over some cardboard boxes and what appeared to be empty orange crates, Bill made it down a dark hallway until he came upon a brightly painted green door that had a cowboy swinging a lasso over his head. Having no doubt that it was the men's room, Bill ventured in.

After bumping into an overflowing trash can, Bill squished his way over to a row of sinks. The hardness of the water had badly stained the once pure white porcelain, but, as bad luck would have it, there was no running water. For that matter, everything in the building was shut off. There was no electricity, no water, and no heat - just cold darkness, except for the shine illuminating from Bill's oversized lantern. The sinks were close enough together to allow Bill to set his lantern down on the edges. He needed to get a closer look at his mud-soaked leg and wanted to take off his waterlogged shoe and sock. Fortunately, there was still plenty of paper in the bathroom – not towels, but toilet paper. "Oh well," thought Bill, "any port in a storm."

Balling up fistfuls of toilet paper, Bill pulled off his shoe and sock and then proceeded to wipe down his foot. With each passing swipe, clots of small paper pieces stuck fast to his skin. It was a small price to pay to get his foot dry. He knew that getting his sock dry, on the other hand, would be a hopeless endeavor, so he sighed heavily and quietly accepted his fate and the demise of his one sock.

Like a basketball player shooting a foul shot, Bill tossed his saturated sock onto the top of the trash can. As the sock landed in its final resting place, the paper in the trash can flew in every direction and floated gently to the bathroom floor. "Well," Bill said out loud, "at least my foot is dryer."

"I'm happy to hear that," came a voice that startled Bill so much that he fell backward, bouncing off a sink and landing flat on his back. Scrambling to get to his feet and holding his searchlight like a billy club, Bill shouted, "Who are you?"

"Take it easy, big fella. My name is Henry. I keep a watch over the building. I saw a faint light and saw that the front door was open, so I came in to check things out. Sorry I startled you. You gave me quite a fright too. May I ask who you are?"

Shaking and still gasping for air, Bill responded, "My name is Bill Richardson. I work for Commercial Retail Properties, and the owners of this building contacted my company."

Bending down to gather himself and to ease his breathing, Bill continued, "I assess buildings like this one all over the country to see what they are worth. The owners want to know what it would take to get this building ready for sale and how much money they might be able to get for it. Wow! You, sir, gave me quite a scare."

"Well, I apologize again for that," said Henry, "but since we closed, I've never seen anyone come back in here. I'm thankful that you didn't whack me in the head with that search flashlight of yours."

"You ought to be thankful. I was getting ready to let you have it."

Henry stood completely still in the doorway, patiently waiting for Bill to recover. He did not want Bill to feel any more uncomfortable than he already did. "What happened to your foot? Do you always walk around dark buildings at night with only one sock and shoe on?" inquired Henry.

Still a little shaken, Bill answered, "I stepped into a pothole the size of a large swimming pool. I survived, but unfortunately, my left shoe and sock did not fare so well."

As his voice started to settle down, Bill lowered his search flashlight and asked, "So. You know a lot about O'Brien's Basket?"

Even in the faint light, Bill could see a slight sparkle in Henry's eyes as he answered warmly, "I should say so. I started here as a stock boy. Every time I come into this old place, I can still smell the apples and fresh baked donuts. Memories of great places always fill your senses."

The Masterful Merchant

Such familiar words got Bill's attention! "Well, you have some powerful memory. What I smell is certainly not apples and donuts."

"Ahhhhh," Henry said as he titled back his head with his eyes closed and gave a long, cheerful sigh. "If you had spent 50 years in this place like I did, you would."

"What happened?", Bill asked curiously. "Why did this business not make it?" It was a question he had asked himself a thousand times in hundreds of closed stores.

Henry paused for a moment and then responded, "Well, there are probably a lot of reasons. I have my own opinions about what happened. I think when the business was sold to some new folks they forgot to pay attention to the seven principles. The old man used to call them the "seven **P**'s."

"The seven **P**'s? What are the seven **P**'s?" Bill thought he had asked the question silently to himself, but then Henry answered.

"The seven **P**'s are what every Masterful Merchant knows. They are what Mr. O'Brien taught me. What old man O'Brien tried to teach everyone."

Bill could hear the affection in Henry's voice. He could tell the words "old man" were meant to be an endearing description of a man Henry loved and admired.

"Ok, now I have two questions," Bill's voice cracked a bit in frustration.

"What are the seven **P**'s and what is a Masterful Merchant?"

"Well," Henry sighed, "Old man O'Brien was a Masterful Merchant. But if you really want to understand what made him a Masterful Merchant and what the seven **P**'s are all about, you'd really have to see for yourself."

"Now how in the world am I supposed to do that? Is old man O'Brien still around? Is he lurking behind the deli counter?"

With a calm voice, Henry said, "No, Mr. O'Brien is long gone.

But I think I can help you discover on your own the answers to your questions. Just take a look into that mirror in front of you. Go on. Take a good, long look."

Bill wasn't interested in looking into some dingy cracked mirror, especially not in the faint light of a lantern and certainly not with some old coot standing in a dark abandoned restroom. It was starting to feel a bit weird and uncomfortable, so Bill declined.

"Look, Charlie, or Henry, or whatever your name is. I have a lot to do, so I really don't have time to reflect on my reflection. Now if you will excuse me, I have to go back to work."

As direct and impolite as his answer was, Henry just stood still, calmly looking at Bill. He had met a lot of people named Bill over his lifetime, many during his 50 years at O'Brien's Basket. Henry just knew how to listen to people. He had this knack for making people feel comfortable.

Henry's polite, easy manner and soothing voice were complimented by the way he dressed. Even in the poor light of his lantern, Bill could see that Henry paid attention to his appearance. Henry's clothes were clean and well-pressed. His gray hair was neatly trimmed and combed. His shoes had a military shine, which seemed very in line with the way Henry stood. So straight and proud.

But what stood out most about Henry was his smile. The kind of smile that fills up the entire face. The kind of smile that shows through eyes of wisdom and grace. The kind of smile that tells you he has knowledge valiantly earned through years of experience.

"Are you sure you don't want to take a few minutes to get the answers to your questions?" Henry said to Bill in a calm but commanding voice.

The change in Henry's tone gave Bill a sense that he was with a man who was much more than a 'stock boy.' He admitted to himself that he was intrigued by what Henry said about O'Brien being a Masterful

Merchant. He wanted to know what the seven **P**'s were all about. He wanted to understand more about what had happened to the store.

"Ok," Bill declared, still sounding a bit annoyed, but more embarrassed for his earlier outburst. Balling up some more of his favorite toilet paper, Bill wiped the surface of the mirror and leaned forward.

"So what is it you want me to see other than my tired face and red eyes?"

"Just take a look. I want you to see the face of a Masterful Merchant."

Leaning even closer, Bill saw Henry's face slowly emerge in the mirror taking the place of his own face. A blinding light exploded out of the mirror, forcing Bill to slam shut his eyes. He could feel his feet lift off the ground as he was being pulled into the mirror.

"What's happening?" shouted Bill as he covered both eyes with his trembling hands. "What's happening? Help me! Help me, Henry!"

CHAPTER TWO

Discovering the First Principle

"**H**ELP ME! HELP!" The deafening sound of his voice echoed in his ears as Bill desperately tried to keep his feet on the ground. Swirling and spinning, Bill felt his body flying through space. The sensation was tearing at him like the first sudden drop on a roller-coaster ride. Bill kept yelling and kept his eyes slammed shut. He had no idea what was happening to him when in, an instant, everything stopped. With a jolt, Bill's feet hit the floor.

He slowly opened his eyes, and, as they adjusted to the bright lights, Bill could hear voices all around him. He realized he was still standing in a restroom. Only now the room was new and the store was filled with people, happy people. People talking to each other, having the kind of conversations you would have with a backyard neighbor.

The restroom was sparkling. It was so clean you could, as old man O'Brien was fond of saying, "eat off the floor." Every sink had bright chrome faucets, the old fashioned kind with long sweeping necks and individual handles. Wicker baskets with O'Brien's logo proudly lined the shelves above the sinks where they caressed brown paper towels. The trash cans were wooden crates lined with hay. The lightly stained concrete floors perfectly balanced the black and white wall tile. And on every wall there were signs promoting the daily specials.

The signs were written in crayon and you could tell by the simple handwriting that the authors were children. One sign said, "Apple Cimminin Donuts Are The Best!" Another said, "I love the fresh smell of Punkin Pie." Bill knew the heartfelt meaning in the messages. His stomach growled as he read a few more slightly misspelled, but appetizing words.

Leaning over the pure white porcelain sink, Bill slowly looked up and could not believe what he saw. It was his face, but he looked so much younger. He had on a gleaming white apron with his name embroidered on it. Underneath his name was a hand drawn wicker basket logo with the name "O'Brien's Basket" stitched proudly across the center.

"Hey Bill! Com' on. Let's go. The old man is walking the back of the store and wants to talk to all the stock boys." The words vibrated in Bill's ears. They came from the mouth of a tall young man who wore the same embroidered O'Brien's Basket apron. He had perfectly creased pants. His shoes sparkled like the sun and his hair was neatly trimmed and combed. He stood in the restroom doorway so proud and tall with a smile that made the room seem even brighter.

"Excuse me. Who are you?" Bill said, almost in disbelief, like he was in a dream.

"Whadda ya, mean? Who am I? It's me, Henry. Come on. Stop kiddin' around. Let's go!"

Bill stood still in amazement. "Could this young, energetic person be that old man Henry?" he said to himself. But before he could ask another question, he felt a strong tug on his sleeve as Henry pulled him out the door of the restroom and into the store.

And what a store! Customers everywhere. Rows and rows of customers. From the restroom door, Bill could see all the way to the front of the store. He could see customers standing 5 to 6 deep at every register and people in white aprons scurrying everywhere. On the walls, he could see poster sized photos of children eating watermelon and of grandparents sharing chocolate with their grandchildren.

Before Bill could soak it all in, Henry yanked his arm once again and pulled him back toward the receiving area. There a large man stood bigger than life. He had a neatly trimmed, snowy white beard and if not for his bald head, you would think he was Santa Claus in a white apron.

"Ok, O'Brien's best!", he bellowed in a jovial voice. "Today we are featuring Mom's Fresh Baked Pies. Let's make sure we keep all the shelves filled. Henry, you make sure all the sample trays have plenty of pieces of pie. We want to keep our customers' taste buds smiling. And Bill, you make sure that the barrels of fresh milk drinks stay filled with ice. Make sure you keep enough cartons of chocolate milk in them for the kids."

Bill realized that old man O'Brien was talking directly to him. Without thinking, he turned to Henry and said, "How does old man O'Brien know me? Am I in some sort of dream? How did I get here, Henry? Why am I so young?"

Henry smiled; the kind of smile that fills up the entire face. And even though this was a much younger looking Henry, he still had the kind of smile that shows through eyes of wisdom and grace. Bill could feel it even when he looked at the 'young' Henry. With reassuring words, Henry said, "You wanted to know what a Masterful Merchant was. You wanted to know about the seven **P**'s. Does it really matter how you got here? Does it really matter if this is a dream? I can assure you, this place and all the people in it are real...very real. Now is your chance to discover the answers to both questions. Come on. Let's go talk to old man O'Brien."

Still feeling a bit bewildered, Bill followed as quickly as he could, but had trouble keeping up with Henry's long strides. The next thing he heard was Henry cheerfully shouting, "Mr. O'Brien, Mr. O'Brien."

A fatherly response immediately came back, "Please, call me Pat," as O'Brien turned realizing the voice he heard was not a customer's, but Henry's.

"Oh! Henry. It's you. I thought you were a customer. What can I do for you, my fine young lad?"

"Well sir, Bill is new here and..." Before Henry could say another word, O'Brien interrupted him and said, "I know who Bill is. I know all my associates. How are you doing today, Bill?"

Taken aback, but with a certain sense of inward pride that old man O'Brien knew who he was, Bill sheepishly answered, "I guess I'm ok, sir."

"YOU GUESS!" The words rumbled out of O'Brien like a freight train. Laughing that deep Santa laugh, O'Brien grabbed Bill on the shoulder and said, "Look around you, Bill. What do you see?"

"Ah - - well. Do you mean in the store?" Bill's uncertainty on how to answer such a simple question made him feel a little embarrassed. He was still trying to grasp the reality of his situation.

"It's not a tough question, son. Tell me what you see."

Looking around, Bill whispered, "Well...."

"Speak up, son! Put a little more voice behind that voice of yours."

A firm slap on the back jump-started Bill, and in a much louder voice he said, "I see a lot of people. I see signs and products and employees. I see cash registers and shopping carts."

"Can you see yourself?" interrupted O'Brien.

"What do you mean?" Bill asked.

"Well, step outside with me. Come on, Henry. Join us."

Walking through the store took what seemed like hours. O'Brien stopped every few feet to greet customers and help them put products in their bright green shopping carts. He oozed sincerity with every hello, every pat on a young child's head, and every look into a customer's eye. He knew every customer by first name and they knew him.

When they finally stepped outside, Bill was quick to notice the dark, abandoned parking lot where his foot had met a watery grave was now a beautifully landscaped oasis for cars. The perfectly lined pavement and pristine blacktop were a stark contrast to the pothole-ridden nightmare Bill had driven on the night before. Or was it the night before?

The only one who walked more briskly than Henry was O'Brien. Bill had trouble again keeping up, but he really did not have much choice. O'Brien tugged at him harder than Henry did. Now he faced the same ritual outside the store as he did inside the store.

O'Brien stopped at every car, helping old and young alike put their bags of groceries in the trunks and back seats. Every customer got a big hello and a bigger thank you. "Don't worry about that cart," he would cheerfully say to each patron, "We'll take care of it." And without any hesitation, the old man would gallop back to the front of the store, pushing carts in front of him.

"Too many carts sitting out in the parking lot. Go grab as many as you can, men. People can't shop if they don't have carts. They need to be up in the front of the store where our customers can get them. Come on. Let's Go!"

And with that, Henry and Bill followed O'Brien's lead, grabbing as many carts as they could and pushing them in a long row to the corral by the front entrance. Bill took it as a challenge to keep up with Henry. To customers, it must have looked like a race to see who could move the most carts in the shortest time...nothing better than a friendly competition to get the blood flowing.

Energized and wiping beads of sweat off his brow, Bill turned his attention back to O'Brien and said in a much stronger voice, "What did you mean when you said, 'Can you see yourself?'"

O'Brien answered "I always look for people who can see themselves in others. If you did not see me greeting customers, stopping to help them, pushing carts and looking into their eyes to thank them, would you have even noticed them? My question was meant to get you to stop and always see yourself through others."

Before saying anything more, O'Brien flew past Bill and greeted another customer who was loading her car, "Let me get that, Mrs. Patterson."

Henry watched in admiration as his mentor sprinted back toward the front of the store, eagerly pushing Mrs. Patterson's empty shopping cart. Glancing over at Bill, Henry said, "What do you see now?"

"I see a man who cares about people. And I see lots of people who care about that man."

Bill's words came out in a slow, measured tone. He knew what Pat O'Brien meant when he asked, "Can you see yourself?" He knew that O'Brien could see himself in the eyes and smiles of every customer. He knew that his passion, caring and enthusiasm behind everything he did was reflected back at him through his customers.

"I also see a Masterful Merchant," Bill reflected, almost to himself.

"You've only seen a small part of being a Masterful Merchant. An important part, but you really haven't seen anything yet," Henry responded. "Tell me, what else you have learned so far?"

Staring at O'Brien like a star struck kid, Bill answered, "I think I've discovered the first Principle. It's **People**. Everything I've seen so far revolves around People."

"Anything else?" asked Henry.

"I think Mr. O'Brien wants us to learn how to make sure customers are the most important People. I think he wants us to put them first, to make sure everything we do at O'Brien's Basket is for their benefit."

Henry continued, "What else do you think the old man wanted you to learn?"

Bill pondered the question only for a moment, "I think...no...I know that to work at O'Brien's Basket, you have to love helping customers in everything you do. The old man does it with every word and every action. I've never seen anyone enjoy serving customers more than he does."

"Not so hard, is it? The first principle every Masterful Merchant understands is People. Not only having the right People as employees, but understanding that all customers are People and all People are different."

"At 'The Basket,'" the nickname that employees were fond of saying, "*We have been taught that every customer is different, so we try to treat every customer the way they want to be treated.*"

"Look at that busy, harried executive over there," Henry instructed Bill. "He wants to just blast in and blast out of the store. O'Brien's Best are People who know how to recognize that customer type. We have to make sure we help him get what he needs in a hurry."

"Sweet little Mrs. Sanders over there has been shopping at the Basket for over 40 years. She loves the attention and has plenty of time to talk while she shops. O'Brien put in several park style benches throughout the store just for customers like her. Tommy Carlyle, our delivery boy, brings her groceries to her home every week. Despite his insistence that he does not want her to tip him, Mrs. Sanders always gives Tommy two dollars."

Henry motioned over to a young couple chasing down twins in aisle 12, the candy aisle. "Robbie and Joan Walsh are always here on Saturday morning with their twins in tow. They like having one of O'Brien's Best help keep a watchful eye on their kids. Mattie and Max love the play area and we keep it staffed to make sure the kids stay safe."

"I guess the best lesson for me," said Bill, "is to take care of People the way each one prefers to be taken care of. Mr. O'Brien is showing how to do this with every customer."

"So, want to learn more?", asked Henry. But before Bill could answer, he heard that bellowing laugh that Pat O'Brien was so famous for.

The old man had climbed aboard one of two riding horses that guarded the front entrance, slapping his thigh as he challenged his rival and her horse to a pretend race. The grin on the young child's face got wider and wider as O'Brien whooped and hollered. "I think you got me, Pardner!" declared O'Brien as he hopped down from his saddle. "Come on inside and let me buy you a drink."

With a wave of his big arm, the little cowgirl galloped into the store with her parents following close behind. Bill noticed that there was duct tape covering both coin slots on the horsey rides. Henry said, "Mr. O'Brien would never charge the 25 cents most places get. He always felt that the free ride and the free soda he occasionally bought for a customer's child would pay off many times over."

Watching as O'Brien and his little friend disappeared inside the store, Bill was convinced that business had nothing to do with why the old man jumped on that horse.

CHAPTER THREE

Building a G.O.R. Culture

Before heading back inside the store, Bill found himself gathering up a few more carts. "Customers can't shop if they don't have carts!" he said silently to himself. "Whoa!" Bill exclaimed as he coiled back from the cold, wet chill against his neck. Spinning quickly around, he saw the old man playfully holding a can of soda. "That always wakes people up!" O'Brien laughed. "Come with me. Let's enjoy our drinks before going back inside. Do you know how to walk a store, Bill?"

Bill wanted to say, "Yeah, one foot in front of the other", but he thought better than to give a glib answer. Instead, he politely said, "I'm not sure what you mean, Mr. O'Brien."

"You always walk a store with a customer's eye. You have to see what they see, every time you walk a store. I have a rule that cannot be broken at The Basket. My store must be G.O.R. everyday!"

G.O.R.? What is G.O.R.? Must be some kind of secret "Basket" code, thought Bill. But before he could ask, O'Brien jumped in. "G.O.R. is Grand Opening Ready! Do you know what I mean by that, Bill?"

Feeling a bit more confident, Bill answered, "I think it means that a store should look as good as the first day it opened. Everything is clean, neat and orderly, everything in its place." Bill looked at O'Brien the way a young school boy looks at his teacher, waiting to get complimented in front of the whole class.

Instead, O'Brien shouted, "Is that the best you can come up with? I've seen a lot of clean, neat and...what was it you said?...'orderly' stores. Most of them bore me to death. Stores that are clean, neat and safe are definitely a part of being Grand Opening Ready. But there is so much more to G.O.R."

"Let's step inside the front entrance and take a look." O'Brien said as he tugged on Bill's sleeve once again. "What do you see, Bill?"

Bill rattled off the usual list of answers...clean store, lots of product, good lighting. But after about three seconds, O'Brien turned to Henry and said, "Henry, what do you see?"

Without hesitation Henry said, "I see 'WOW' everywhere. I see the right products in the right quantities in the right places in the store. I see signs that tell me as a customer right where to go to find what I am looking for. I see white aprons milling with customers."

"It's a visual feast. Everything in this store excites all my senses. The sights, the sounds and the smells. I can feel the energy in here. My taste buds are exploding, and I can't wait to bite into a free sample." Henry was now smiling ear to ear and, if not for the noise of busy customers, you could have heard his stomach rumbling.

"That's very good, Henry. But there is still much more to G.O.R. Look over there where the fresh flowers are...what do you see?"

"I see a lot of pretty flowers," Bill blurted out the words like an anxious student.

O'Brien laughed and said, "You're right, Bill. And they better be pretty, or we won't sell any. What I see are arrangements perfectly presented with elegant wrappings and a variety of sizes and prices to appeal to the widest range of customers. What I see are O'Brien's Best people cheerfully helping people with their purchase decision. What

I see are O'Brien's Best people carefully tending to delicate plants, plants of all different types and sizes. Look how they cascade down the wall in a waterfall of colors."

As he talked, the lines in the old man's face seem to vanish. You would swear the more O'Brien talked, the younger he looked. Even without speaking, you could see in his eyes how much he loved his store. How much he loved "O'Brien's Best" people. How much he loved his customers.

Before Bill could ask O'Brien any questions, the old man was off again, dashing toward the service counter to help another customer. Henry was over by the potted plants carefully stacking bags of soil and making sure all the price tags were correctly and clearly visible to the customers.

"Hey Bill," Henry called out. "Run back to receiving and ask Franklin, our receiving manager, for a carton of women's gardening gloves and a box of the Scott's hand shovels, the kind used for planting flowers. He'll know what you mean. Go on, hurry up."

Bill took off in the direction of the back of the store, quickening his space with every step. Like a man on a mission, he flew past customers, not seeing or hearing a thing. That is until Mrs. Sanders stopped him dead in his tracks with her walker.

"Where's the fire, young man?" said Mrs. Sanders in her Sunday school voice.

"I'm sorry. I have to get some things out from the shipping area," said Bill, sounding a bit winded.

"Well, my good fellow. You almost ran over little Max, and I'm sure his mother could have used a little help from you loading that sack of potatoes into her shopping cart," Mrs. Sanders said as she pointed back toward the child.

The words coming from Mrs. Sander's voice were not harsh or criticizing. She sounded more like a caring and nurturing grandmother, offering a small piece of sage advice.

"Maybe you ought to run back down to little Max and ask his mother if there is anything you could help her with?" Bill hesitated at first, wanting to tell Mrs. Sanders that he had to get product out to the floor, but instead, he headed back down the aisle.

"I'm sorry, ma'am. Let me get that bag for you. Is there anything else I can help you with?" A bright, pleasant smile, was followed by a, "Thank you very much. I have everything, but it's so nice of you to ask." The young mother read his name that was embroidered across his white apron and added, "I have not see you around here, Bill."

"I'm new here, ma'am," came the reply from Bill.

"Well welcome. My name is Joan. Joan Walsh. And that little scamp over there is my son, Max. My daughter, Maggie, is playing in the play area. They love coming here. All of O'Brien's people are so helpful and so nice. You are going to like it here."

After a few more words, Bill thanked Joan and headed back toward shipping, getting a nod of approval from Mrs. Sanders.

Bill had lost track of time and had waited on several customers before finally returning to meet Henry, with women's gardening gloves and hand shovels in tow.

With a knowing look, Henry said, "Got caught up helping out customers, didn't you?"

"Well, it's hard not to when, every few feet, they come up and ask for something. It started to get a little annoying, especially since I really don't know where anything is in the store. I also didn't want to keep you waiting so long."

"I had plenty to do and plenty of customers to wait on," responded Henry in his calm, soothing voice. "You should never feel that waiting on customers is annoying. That is what O'Brien's Best live for. Customers always come first. Let's get this product properly displayed. People who buy potted plants need gardening gloves and hand shovels. The old man believes that a Masterful Merchant has a responsibility to help customers buy everything they need and make it as convenient as possible. Some retailers call it cross merchandising. Mr. O'Brien calls it caring for customers."

Bill found himself soaking in every word that Henry spoke. He was starting to understand that Grand Opening Ready everyday started with the first **P**, People. People who were "O'Brien's Best."

People who are so in tune with their customers always do the right thing, even when no one was looking or asking them. O'Brien's Best represented a G.O.R. culture..."treat everyday like Grand Opening Day!" Take care of customers first.

Most people though that keeping a store well stocked with the right products in the right places and clearly priced was the best way to take care of customers. In O'Brien's world, the best way to show your customer you respect their valuable time and money, was to always make sure every inch of the store and every person in the store was Grand Opening Ready...Everyday!

Bill had an idea what the second **P** was all about, but to be sure he leaned over his gardening shovels and asked Henry, "So, are you going to tell me what the second **P** is all about, or do I still have to guess?"

"Well," Henry said with a drawn out sigh, "If you haven't discovered it yet on your own, then you might not have what it takes to be a Masterful Merchant."

"Whoever said I even wanted to be a Masterful Merchant? I didn't ask to come here!"

Getting angrier, Bill burst out, "One minute I'm standing in a dark and dingy bathroom, and then I'm pulled through a mirror, and then I......." but before Bill could finish his sentence, a blinding light hit him.

Bill felt his body lift off the ground. He was being pulled higher and higher but could not see anything around him. His eyes were too watery and still stinging from the flash of light. His body started to spin and twirl. He felt out of control. But just as quickly as his unexpected journey started, it ended with a sudden thump.

Bill found himself sitting on a cold concrete floor. There was darkness all around him, but he could sense he was back in the dirty restroom of the old abandoned building, although this time he was all alone.

CHAPTER FOUR

The Second and Third Principles Revealed

Feeling disoriented, Bill stood up and steadied himself against one of the stained sinks. His lantern was still sitting like a solitary lighthouse, giving off enough light for Bill to grab his duffle bag and make his way out of the restroom door and toward the front of the store. The thoughts swirling through his head kept his mind off the soreness in his backside caused by his abrupt contact with the solid restroom floor.

Squeezing his body and his oversized duffle through the front entrance, Bill pushed the door shut and reached into his bag for the monster key ring. Again, with a magician's touch, he produced the right key and locked the door. When he reached his rental car, Bill opened the trunk and set his duffle down. He felt like a wounded soldier, weary and troubled by all that he just went through, uncertain if it was real.

With his tools and lantern all safely packed away, Bill climbed into his car and started the engine. "WHOA!", gasped Bill in a shaken voice loud enough to wake the dead. His hands trembled on the steering wheel as he looked at the outline of a man standing in front of his car.

Startled, Bill slammed the car into reverse. The tires squealed as he sped away. The harsh shadows created by the car's headlights started to grow as he drove farther and farther away from the imposing figure.

The car bounced violently over one of the concrete medians, causing both back tires to explode. Bill whipped his head around to look over his shoulder. His heart pounded even harder in his chest when he saw a man sitting in the back seat. He rammed the car into park and jumped out the door, running as fast as his legs would carry him.

"Bill! Bill! Stop. It's me, Henry," a familiar voice echoed across the parking lot.

Not trusting his own ears and not certain of anything, Bill kept running. He headed back toward the front of the store wishing he had not locked the door. Winded and frightened, his frantic running slowed until finally, Bill reached the entrance to the building.

There in front of him was Henry, standing tall and proud. "Bill. It's me, Henry. Take it easy. You don't have to be afraid."

Leaning over and grasping both knees, Bill shouted, "What are you trying to do, give me a heart attack? You stay away from me! You're not real. This is not real. I don't know what's happening, but get away from me. Leave me alone!"

Henry did not move or say anything. He stood still in the doorway and waited patiently for Bill to recover. He realized that this was the second time he had given Bill quite a startle, so it was easy to understand how Bill was feeling. But Henry also knew Bill had a certain passion about retailing and he still had so many unanswered questions. He knew how valuable Bill could be to others.

"What do you want from me?" Bill finally said in desperate voice.

"First, I want you to settle down. I apologize and I promise I will never frighten you again. I only want to help you find the answers to your questions."

Henry had such a fatherly way about him. He spoke in a manner that made you instantly feel comfortable and safe. Somehow, despite all that was happening, Bill sensed he could trust Henry.

"My heart is racing so fast, I can't even remember my questions," Bill asserted in a still breathless voice.

"You wanted to know what made a Masterful Merchant. You wanted to know about the seven **P**'s," Henry reminded Bill.

"If I have to go through much more of this – then I'm not sure I want to know. It's not worth it!" Bill sounded emphatic as he slowly rose up to look at Henry.

With a smile that shown through the eyes of wisdom and grace, Henry approached Bill. "Every Masterful Merchant faces their fears everyday. They are risk taking, self-made people who put everything they have into what they do. They go through a lot of pain and joy and, sometimes, suffering. In the end, however, the Masterful Merchants know it's all worth it."

Feeling more at ease and having caught his breath, Bill couldn't ignore his curiosity. He wanted to go back to The Basket. He wanted to understand more about the seven **P**'s. "So, did it take you 50 years to learn how to be a Masterful Merchant?"

Without responding, Henry motioned for Bill to follow him into the dark store. Bill did not even notice the front entrance was unlocked as he walked toward Henry and squeezed past the door frame, leaving his damaged car and its contents unceremoniously perched on the median outside.

In an instant, Bill was standing in The Basket, all bright, new and shiny. Grand Opening Ready! Customers and O'Brien's Best were milling around in every direction. Bill could hear the old man's voice in the distance, "Here you go, Mrs. Fisher."

"Hey Bill. Whadda yah think of that presentation?" O'Brien beamed as he motioned for Henry and Bill to come over to the mountain of Sissy's Sarsaparilla. The rich, dark six packs of brown bottles were stacked perfectly in a stair step fashion, running all the way up the end-cap from the floor to the ceiling.

"SSS, Henry. SSS, that's the key!" O'Brien said as he gave Henry a swift pat on the back and headed down the center aisle to help another customer.

"SSS? What's SSS?" Bill looked like he was talking out loud to himself. With a knowing smile, Henry said, "Safely Secure and Sale-able!"

"O'Brien wants every product presented in a secure and safe manner, and he wants every product to be sale-able. Show every product in a way that creates in every customer an 'appetite to buy', as the old man is so fond of saying."

"Presentation! That's the second Principle." The words flew out of Bill's mouth. He threw out his chest while Henry politely clapped his hands, acknowledging what Bill discovered.

"Very good, Bill. But Presentation is not as easy as it sounds. Although O'Brien wants every presentation to create a great first impression, he also wants every presentation to make sense, and to ensure that the rule of SSS is never violated. Safely Secure and Sale-able."

"Presentation is also all about the details," continued Henry. "Price tags that are clearly visible. Cross-merchandised products like the cups and straws nearby. That's how The Basket shows it cares for customers. Look at the storyboard over there and how it adds a human touch about Sissy, the person behind the product. Can you see how much fun Ginny is having serving customers a sip of Sissy's Sarsaparilla? Customers sure seem to enjoy it."

"As a Masterful Merchant, Bill, you also have to know what Product makes sense. At The Basket, we don't put window fans on sale in the winter. The Sarsaparilla is the right product for summer, especially since Sissy's is celebrating their 100th Anniversary. Customers love the nostalgia behind the story as much as they love the taste of the product. Another thing The Old Man insists on... A I S."

"AIS...SSS...GOR? Boy, O'Brien sure uses a lot of acronyms. He has initials for everything."

"Well, not quite everything," declared Henry.

Bill wished he had his notebook and his favorite pen to jot down notes, but they were stowed away deep in his duffle bag. He wondered for a moment if he'd ever see them or his rental car again.

Henry continued, "O'Brien's Best knows the important initials and what they mean. O'Brien uses simple acronyms to make it easier to remember what we all need to do to be Masterful Merchants.

"Safely Secure and Sale-able," said Henry, drawing the letters in the air with his finger. "SSS reminds us to keep our product selections presented in a safe manner so our customers never get injured. AIS, Always In Stock, reminds us that customers cannot buy product if it's not on the shelf. AIS is the key to providing world class customer service and to being Grand Opening Ready, everyday."

"How about TRP?," asked Bill.

"Do you mean The Right Product?" Henry replied with a sly grin on his face. "That's part of *Merchandising 101*; the Right Product presented at the Right Time in the Right Place with the Right Quantities at the Right Price."

"And," chimed in Bill, "Presented by the Right People. People who care about customers. People, Presentation, and Product. That's three Principles. That's three **P**'s. What's the fourth?"

In mid-sentence, Henry's response to Bill's question was muffled by the thunderous boom of a bass drum. Marching from the front of the store were 20 band members from the local high school. Their bright green uniforms were topped off by large blooms of emerald feathers floating down from their white rimmed hats. Two by two, they

51

streamed to the front of the store with Old Man O'Brien joining the parade.

With horns raised and drum sticks ready, the band started to play "Happy Birthday to You" in a rather unusual but catchy way. "Happy Birthday to You. Boom! Boom! Happy Birthday to You. Boom! Boom!" All the customers moved closer to the front of the store waiting in anticipation for the next verse. Whose birthday were they celebrating?

"Happy Birthday Sissy Sarsaparilla. Boom! Boom! Happy Birthday to You."

"Free Drinks for Everyone!" shouted O'Brien. Customers clapped and cheered as white apron clad O'Brien's Best people handed out cold, icy bottles of soda. A Happy 100th Birthday Banner dropped down from the ceiling followed by dozens of colorful balloons.

"Pat, you never cease to amaze me," said Mrs. Sanders.

"Well," said Pat, "your mother Sissy always amazed me. She sent me my first order when I opened. I had very little money, but she took me at my word that I would pay her. I'll never forget what she did to help me get started."

"And I'll never forget what you have done for me and for my company over all these years, Pat. You are a Masterful Merchant." O'Brien's fair Irish complexion turned a light shade of pink. He was clearly embarrassed by the compliment. With a whispered "Thank You" and a gentle shake of the hand, O'Brien returned to what he loved...waiting on his customers.

CHAPTER FIVE

The Ultimate Promoter

"**H**enry! Bill! Help out Stephanie and Peggy on the registers. Can't keep our customers waiting too long."

Henry sprinted to the first cashier and started bagging groceries, glancing up to see Bill still standing and staring at Mr. O'Brien. "Come on Bill. Our customer's time is valuable. Help out Peggy."

Bill ran quickly over to the second register and started furiously packing products into the brown, stenciled O'Brien's Basket bags. "Thank You, Bill," said Peggy. "It's been a great day. Don't you just love having so many customers to help? I love it when we are this busy." There was no doubting Peggy's sincerity. She loved waiting on customers.

Not wanting to slow down the customer's checkout, Bill kept rifling products into bag after bag. Stacking them carefully into a shopping cart, he glanced over at Henry and gave a little smile as if to say, "Hey, I beat you." Henry did not mind. He actually enjoyed seeing the look on Bill's face.

Bill's moment of triumph was short lived, however, when O'Brien came up behind him and said, "Do you know how many years loyal feet have stood at these registers helping customers? Peggy makes me proud everyday!"

O'Brien's words sank deep into Bill. It was the same question he had asked himself when he first saw the rows of old cash registers on top of checkout stands covered by dirt and piles of faded register tapes. The words brought back vivid images of the abandoned store. Bill could not understand how a vibrant place like The Basket could end up going out of business.

Sounding like a proud Papa, O'Brien turned and headed out the front entrance to help another customer. Anxious to learn more, Bill followed in quick pursuit. He did not notice the high school band members lining the front windows with crisp new posters promoting "The King and I". He also did not notice the customer struggling with her shopping cart, but Henry did. Henry was always aware of the customers.

With one quick jerk, Henry dislodged the cart. "There you go, ma'am. Enjoy your day and thank you for coming to The Basket."

Turning his attention back toward Bill, Henry saw that he had caught up to O'Brien and was helping him load a customer's car. Without a word, Bill instinctively sprinted back toward the front of the store, rushing to get the empty cart back in the corral. Flying past Henry, he shouted, "Customers can't shop without a cart!"

"Come on, Henry," O'Brien said as he watched the old man wrap his arm around Bill's neck, the way coaches do with their football players. Every word that O'Brien said and everything he did taught Henry so much. Just being with him, if only for a few minutes each day, was such a great learning experience.

"It's like P.T. Barnum once said, *'Customers won't buy a thing if they don't know what you're selling'*." Henry could never find that quote anywhere, but it did not matter. The old man was preaching and teaching and loved to use sayings as much as initials and acronyms to get his point across.

"You have to always be promoting something people want. You have to do it in a way that is better than your competition!" O'Brien was on a roll. His eyes lit up as his speech got faster. The more he talked, the more animated he became. He was the ultimate promoter.

"Bill, we just got in a shipment of Ball Park franks. It's baseball season. A lot of families will be sitting on bleachers watching their little ones play baseball. There will be a lot of picnics and barbeques. Summer time is great! You and Henry go back to receiving and get a bunch of franks so we can start selling to our customers. And set up that old fashioned charcoal grill out front. Let's feed some hungry customers and their kids."

O'Brien beamed as he turned and gave Bill a quick fatherly slap on the back. Then off he went to wait on more customers.

Bill turned to Henry and said with a Cheshire cat grin, "I know the fourth **P**. Everything that makes this place so special is how People Present the right Products and Promote them in a way that creates... what did the old man say... 'an appetite to buy'."

Henry smiled, "Keep that up, Bill, and you might become a Masterful Merchant someday." Glancing back toward the potted plants, Henry said, "Hmmm...we need to bring out some of our copper watering cans and stack them near the potting soil."

CHAPTER SIX

The Simplicity of
BEST - BETTER - GOOD

Bill scurried to catch up to Henry as they headed back toward receiving. He could not conceal the sense of pride swelling inside him created by his new found knowledge. "People, Presentation, Product, and Promotion." The words kept playing over and over again inside his head.

Never before had Bill felt so filled with excitement. His mind was swirling with ideas. He couldn't wait to merchandise the hot dogs and show Mr. O'Brien. "Let's go!" Bill called out, giving Henry a friendly slap on the back as he raced past him toward receiving.

The freezer in the receiving area was as big as a tennis court. Hundreds of frozen products lined the stainless steel shelves, but everything was organized so that each item could be found quickly and taken out to the floor of the store.

While loading boxes of hot dogs onto a wooden pallet, Bill turned to Henry and said, "Where do I find the hot dog rolls, relish, mustard and ketchup? And do we sell BBQ grills and charcoal? How about all the plastic cups, paper plates, forks, knives? What about picnic baskets?"

"Whoa – slow down, Cowboy! What's got you so ramped up?" Henry said with a knowing grin.

"Presentation! Product! Promotion!"

"And don't forget...People!" Henry said, grinning from ear to ear as he watched Bill pull his treasure of products out the receiving area door and head to the front of the store.

Henry soon followed with a pallet full of complimentary products. "So, how do you think we should position and price these hot dogs?" Henry asked Bill.

"I don't know how to position or price them. And what do you mean by position?" inquired Bill.

"Every Masterful Merchant understands the simplicity of positioning merchandise."

"Since I am obviously not a Masterful Merchant, I don't understand the 'simplicity' of positioning merchandise," Bill responded in a way that showed his frustration.

"Think of positioning first in terms of BEST-BETTER-GOOD. For example, any product that comes in multiple sizes should have price tiers that are logical to the customers.

"For example, we sell four types of hotdogs, available in three sizes, and packaged in small, medium and large quantities. Presenting each product by price is easy. Customers get it when you price products as BEST-BETTER-GOOD. By following a logical step up or step down pricing model, customers can easily compare products and prices. At the Basket, we always want our customers to see the BEST product first because they deserve the BEST."

"But positioning goes way beyond just BEST-BETTER-GOOD," Henry responded. "Positioning also has to do with the type of product. Does it weigh a lot, or is it light? Is it bulky or small? Should it go up higher on a shelf or down closer to the floor?"

"Positioning," continued Henry, "has to do with identifying your target audience. We don't want our elderly customers like Mrs. Sanders reaching too far or bending too low to find the products they need."

"Positioning has to do with finding the right spot in the store. It has to do with seasonality. You certainly don't want snow shovels sitting on an end-cap in July. Positioning has to do with logical adjacencies and displaying complimentary products close to each other. It makes the shopping experience more convenient for customers, and it puts more money in the cash registers".

"Positioning has to do with how products are priced. Every price must be logical to the customer. The customer has to understand every Product/Price equation."

"Positioning," continued Henry, "is making sure there are enough best selling hotdogs on display and not too many of the ones that don't sell. The Old Man always says if you price your products properly, position them in a logical fashion, and put more of your best sellers on display, you'll sell more. O'Brien's Best know how to keep our best selling items in stock."

After a long pause, Bill looked at Henry and said, "O'Brien's best people present and promote products and position them with the proper prices in order to 'create the appetite to buy' with every customer. Have I got it right?" Bill asked, looking like an anxious student, waiting for an approving word or nod from Henry.

"Well," Henry laughingly responded. "You have most of it right. If you had all of it right, you'd be a Masterful Merchant."

Before Bill could respond, their conversation was interrupted by a loud crash. Customers started shouting, "Oh my God! Somebody call 911!"

Sprinting toward the back of the store, Henry and Bill came upon little Max. His body lay motionless underneath sacks of potatoes that had fallen on him. "MOVE!" shouted O'Brien, as he feverishly threw aside the burlap sacks and started CPR on the little boy. "CALL 911 NOW!"

CHAPTER SEVEN

A Broken Promise

The flashing lights of the ambulance reflected off O'Brien's tear-soaked face as he walked toward Max's mother, Joan. She was shaking as she held her daughter, Mattie.

"I am so sorry," O'Brien whispered in a mournful, desperate sigh. "I am so sorry. This should have never happened. This should have never happened." He repeated the words over and over again. They echoed in his head. A dull, lifeless ache enveloped his body. The bitter tasting tears streaming down his face did not remove the dryness in his throat.

Joan Walsh scurried over to a waiting police car to join her husband for the torturous trip to the hospital. Only time would tell if O'Brien's quick action had saved little Max's life.

"What happened?" asked Bill in disbelief.

"Someone placed a pallet of potato sacks on a top shelf, and it collapsed and fell on little Max." Henry's voice trailed off as he stared at the tile floor and the pile of potato sacks scattered across the aisle.

"Henry," O'Brien muttered in a quiet, exhausted voice, "Let's get this cleaned up. I have to go to the hospital. Watch over things until

I get back. We broke our Promise, Henry. We broke our Promise."

Henry had never heard such despair in the Old Man's voice. He had never seen him walk so slowly. It was as if the weight of the world suddenly fell on O'Brien's shoulders. The energy and passion that flowed out of him with every word and every thing he did was completely gone.

For the first time ever, Henry saw O'Brien completely ignore customers. Their kind words and attempts to console the old man fell on deaf ears.

"What did he mean '*We broke our Promise*'," asked Bill?

Henry didn't answer. He just turned abruptly and said, "Let's clean this up. We have a lot of customers to take care of. We have a Promise to keep."

"What Promise, Henry? If that is the seventh principle, what is the Promise?" Bill implored.

Despite the desperate sound of Bill's voice, Henry ignored him and went about cleaning up the aisle and making sure that every product was safely secured. He was not concerned about whether or not the product was sale-able, and he certainly was not interested in continuing a conversation with Bill. He just wanted to make 100% sure that no one would ever get hurt again while shopping at The Basket.

"Why aren't you talking to me, Henry? Why are you leaving me hanging?" Bill continued to press for answers, as Henry walked passed him and disappeared behind the receiving area doors.

Frustrated and determined, Bill stormed after Henry. He violently flung open the receiving area doors and was immediately surrounded by darkness. The familiar smell of rotted produce and mold pierced his nose. He knew that he was back in the abandoned store.

"HENRY! Where are you? Are you here? Please Henry. You promised you would answer my questions. You promised you would help me discover the secret to being a Masterful Merchant. You are breaking your Promise, Henry!" The words exploded out of Bill as he sank to his knees, exhausted and confused.

CHAPTER EIGHT

The Seventh Principle Revealed

It took some time for Bill to rise to his feet. Covered with dirt and dust, he walked toward the receiving doors groping through the darkness with his hands, hoping he would not run into something or someone. As he pushed through the doors, he could see the faint light from his lantern still emanating from the restroom. It was enough light to provide him a safe path to walk.

Upon entering the restroom, Bill saw the lantern resting on the edges of two rust-stained sinks. Right below the lantern was Bill's old tattered duffle bag. "Hmmm. Why is my bag here? I know I left it in the car."

Too preoccupied with all the events of the day and still wondering about the Promise, Bill quickly turned his thoughts to little Max. He wondered if he was ok. He wondered if he was real. He wondered why Henry ignored him. So many questions with no one to ask...so many questions with no answers.

Bill grabbed the handle of his duffle bag and took a long look in the dingy, cracked mirror, hoping that Henry would appear. Hoping that he would be pulled back into O'Brien's Basket. "Henry, please don't leave me like this," Bill quietly whispered as he leaned closer to the mirror.

This time, however, there would be no Henry. No magical portal that would transport him to The Basket. So Bill turned and headed back out to his rental car, hoping that there was not too much damage.

After the normal struggle with the lock to the front entrance, Bill dropped his enormous key ring into his duffle. He was not looking forward to the walk toward his rental car, knowing that it was perched up on a median between two concrete curbs with both tires flattened.

"What?" Bill said, not believing his own eyes. "How did my car end up here?"

Bill's rental car was exactly where he had left it when he first came into the parking lot. There it was sitting perfectly between two faded white lines. Not a scratch on it and with all the tires fully inflated. "Now how did that happen? I know I slammed into that curb. I know I backed over that median and blew both tires. What a crazy night."

Lost in his own thoughts, Bill did not notice an automobile coming toward him until the flashing lights told him it was a police car. Out from a speaker came a booming voice, "Put down the bag and walk toward the car."

Startled, but a bit relieved, Bill dropped his duffle and walked cautiously toward the patrol car. "Who are you and what are you doing in this parking lot at this time of night?," asked an officer.

Bill could not see the officer due to the blinding search lights pointed directly at him, but he answered, "My name is Bill Richardson. I work for Commercial Retail Properties. The owners of this building asked me to come and assess the property."

"Put both your hands on the hood of the car!" Doing exactly as he was told, Bill waited patiently while the officer called into the station to check out his story.

After what felt like a lifetime, the officer stepped out of his patrol car. Walking up behind Bill, he said in a commanding voice, "Show me your identification."

The Masterful Merchant

Bill took his hands off the hood of the car and slowly reached for his wallet. He pulled out his driver's license. "Here you are, Officer."

"Do you always work at night?" The officer's words were sharp and to the point.

"Not normally, but I was running behind. I have to fly out of town tomorrow, so I thought I would get a start on assessing this property tonight before I checked into my hotel," Bill answered in a trembling voice.

"Well I hope you understand why I had to look into who you are and why I asked what you are doing. I have a promise to the neighbors in this community to keep them safe."

The Officer's words brought Bill back to the question that was haunting him. What was O'Brien's Promise? Why wouldn't Henry talk to him? Why wouldn't Henry answer him?

The Officer walked back and got into his patrol car. After what seemed like an eternity, he returned to Bill and handed him back his driver's license. "Alright," said the officer. "Your story checks out. Do you know how to get to your hotel?"

"Yes, Officer."

Looking toward the abandoned building the officer quietly said, "What a great place this used to be. You should have seen it when my Grandfather owned it."

As his eyes became more accustomed to the darkness, Bill could see the faint outline of the officer's name on his badge. It said Patrick O'Brien.

"I bet he was a great man," said Bill, sounding a bit more relieved.

"He was the best. He was so proud of The Basket. That is what all the people in this town called his store. He was so full of life and nothing made him happier that taking care of his people and his customers. He was so fond of the people that worked with him."

"His employees affectionately called him "the Old Man". He called them "O'Brien's Best." Grandpa always felt like he worked for his employees and that they worked for the customers." The officer's voice trailed off as if he was caught in his own world, reliving the wonderful memories of a bygone past.

"Why did the business close?" Bill asked, hoping that he would get an answer to the question that had been burning inside him.

"About 20 years ago, a little boy was injured inside the store. A careless employee put a pallet of potato sacks in an overhead shelf, and it fell and landed on top of the boy. The employee did not do the one thing that was the most important Promise that Grandpa felt The Basket had to keep with every customer."

Anxious to hear the answer, but even more concerned with the welfare of the little boy, Bill leaned forward. He could tell from the sound of his voice that the officer was still feeling the pain caused by the events of that tragic day. "Did you know the little boy?" he quietly asked the officer.

"Yeah, little Max. On the day of the accident, I watched Grandpa give Max CPR. He saved his life. Max had a very rough go for a few years, but he recovered from his injuries. Today, he is a safety engineer for a large manufacturing company."

Unfortunately, my grandfather never recovered from the accident." The officer turned and walked toward his patrol car with his head hanging down.

"What injuries? I didn't see the Old Man get hurt!" Bill blurted out.

The officer, too caught up in the past, did not even hear Bill. He had already gotten in his car and had started the engine when Bill approached and asked again, "What injuries did your grandfather suffer?"

Rolling down the car window, Office Pat replied, "His injuries were not physical. He could not recover from the broken Promise. It was more than his name on this building. Grandpa had his heart and soul tied to his business, and he vowed that customers would also be Safe and Secure at The Basket. Little Max's injury took the life out of

The Masterful Merchant

the Old Man, so he sold the business to some corporate chain. It was never the same."

"Why?" asked Bill. "What was never the same? What did they do?"

"Well, they ignored the seven principles that the old man used to always preach. He always called them the seven **P**'s. When Grandpa owned the place, his O'Brien's Best employees knew that it took caring People to Present Products and Promote, Price and Position them in a way that would create in every customer what he called 'the appetite to buy.' Above all else, he made sure The Basket adhered to a Promise to show every product in a safe, secure and sale-able manner. Keep that Promise always, so that every customer would feel at home."

"Are you sure you're a police officer? You sound like a pretty Masterful Merchant." asserted Bill.

"Masterful Merchant," the officer said with an amusing tone in his voice. "I have a close family friend that always uses that saying every time we talk about The Basket. He had my grandfather's passion, still does. He loved working in this store. He loved customers."

"I might have been an OK Merchant, but I would never have compared to them. They both had an uncanny knack for getting O'Brien's Best to understand everything it took to win over customers and keep them for life."

"The corny acronyms and the way they took simple concepts and made them even easier to understand and execute really stuck with everyone. Look at me. I've been a cop for over 20 years and I still remember the seven **P**'s," the officer said as he stared through his front windshield at the old building. "Must sound pretty silly to a guy like you?"

"Not at all," said Bill. "As a kid, I used to work at a great old country store. I was too young to understand all the things the owners did to win over customers. Like your grandfather, they created a memorable place to shop. Looking back, I can see very clearly what made that store a success."

"My grandpa knew that when caring People, his O'Brien's Best people, really took time with and interest in customers, and when they made every product SSS, that was the best way to fulfill The Promise."

Trying not to show that he knew what Officer Pat was talking about, Bill asked, "What is SSS?"

"The Old Man used to say," answered Officer Pat, "that every competitor makes a Promise to have the lowest prices, the best service, and the best products. But it's caring People that truly make the difference. People who can truly fulfill every Promise and keep the most important one, keep products SSS...Safely Secure and Saleable."

"The new corporate owners were obviously successful before they came in and took over The Basket. There had to be more reasons that they went out of business than just not executing - - what did you call it? The seven **P**'s?" said Bill emphatically. "Retail is pretty complicated."

"I think it was a series of little changes that slowly eroded away a 'customer first' culture. I remember when the new corporate owners changed the return policy," Officer Pat said, with a disappointed grimace as he stared out into the darkness.

"My grandfather took back everything. He used to say, 'Let's not worry about the one person out of one hundred that will try to take advantage of us. Don't penalize the other ninety-nine good, honest customers because of one bad one.' "

"After he sold and left the business, the new owners would not allow anything to be returned without a valid receipt. After five days, they would not take back anything. The new owners only cared about bottom line, short-term profits. They only cared about cutting expenses and their big bonus checks. They did not care about their customers."

"What else did they do?" Officer O'Brien could tell that Bill's question had a deep sense of urgency.

"They did not value O'Brien's Best. Grandpa always felt it was his people that made The Basket great. The new owners cut the staff to 50% part time and 50% full time. It really destroyed service in the store and ruined morale."

"Well, don't companies have an obligation to make a profit?" Bill responded, almost defensively.

"That was one thing that grandpa never worried about. He always made a profit by paying attention to his people and his customers. He knew how to manage his financials. He knew how to run a profitable business. He knew that making money would take care of itself if everyone believed in and executed the seven principles." Officer Pat sat up straighter and straighter with every word he spoke.

"Where is your grandfather now?" Bill inquired.

"He is resting at the North Hill cemetery on the other side of town. I sure hope he is resting peacefully. We buried him right next to Mrs. Sanders. Her mother, Sissy, helped the old man get started in business."

After a long pause, the officer looked up at Bill and extended his hand. As the two strangers exchanged a firm handshake, they both felt they had somehow known each other for years. "Well, I've gotta get back to work. You be careful and drive safely."

A faint smile came to the officer's face as he stared one more time at the building that housed so many memories of his youth. Bill bent down to look at Officer Pat's face. "Your grandfather is very proud of you, and I know that he is resting peacefully."

With a curious glance, Officer Pat acknowledged Bill's kind words, and, with a tip of his cap, he drove off into the night.

CHAPTER NINE

Two Years Later

"**N**eed a little help on register five," Bill shouted in a cheerful voice as he started plowing groceries into a large burlap sack. It was grand opening week at Patrick's Pride and as the proud new owner, Bill wanted every customer to get special white glove service.

"Thank you, Mrs. Wheeler," said Bill as he plopped open another burlap sack. "I sure wish I had known your mom. I've heard all the great stories about her and your grandmother, Sissy."

"Since this is the third time I have been in here this week, Bill, please call me Joan. It's so great to see a new store inside this building. My mom loved shopping at this store when it was O'Brien's Basket. Looking around, it's hard to believe you didn't know Mr. O'Brien or my mom. It's like seeing his store reborn. He would have been very proud to see what you have done with this place."

"Well, I had a lot of great people tell me all about The Basket and especially how your grandmother helped get The Basket started. I know your grandmother and your mom were two of O'Brien's favorite people. They were so much more than just customers."

"I think most of the people in this neighborhood were so much more than just customers," echoed Joan. "Not too long ago, we were all friends. We loved having The Basket as a community meeting place. Neighbors doing business with neighbors. I sure hope you bring that spirit back."

"We'll give it our best. There is a lot of Pride here at Patrick's. Hopefully people will feel it, but only if we do our jobs right. We have a Promise to fulfill," Bill said proudly.

Joan Wheeler smiled at Bill and gave him a reassuring nod. "I'll never forget how many people from The Basket attended Mom's funeral. When Tommy Carlyle gave her eulogy and then donated all the tips she gave him to the local children's hospital, I know she was smiling down from above."

Bill looked at Joan Wheeler, secretly knowing all about Tommy and the tips he always got from Mrs. Sanders for the deliveries he made to her home. "It must have been quite a lot of money. Tommy worked at The Basket for a long time."

"Oh, there's Mattie. Hi, Mattie," shouted Karen as she closed her register drawer and waved. Mattie was pushing her son Patrick toward the play area. With both hands occupied pushing the stroller, she could only give a quick nod and a breathless, "Hi, Karen. How are you?"

Walking into the store behind Mattie was Officer O'Brien. "Top o' the mornin' to yah, Billy!" The Officer sang out in his slight, but distinctive Irish accent, "Thanks for showing off the Old Man," he said as he pointed over toward an enormous wall past the main entrance to the store.

Mounted on the center of the wall was an old wicker basket shaped picture frame with a photo of Pat O'Brien. Under his photo were the hand written words:

"In Honor of a Masterful Merchant, Patrick S. O'Brien. We take Pride in Keeping Our Promise to You and to All Our Valued Customers."

The Masterful Merchant

Below the words were family photos of Patrick's Pride –the proud families of the people who worked at the store. Each smiling face gave you a sense that this special place was truly all about family. Like Joan Wheeler said, "Neighbors doing business with neighbors."

"Hi Honey. How's our little boy?" Officer O'Brien asked his young bride as she put Patrick Junior down on the soft mats in the children's play area. "When he gets bigger, he's going to think this store was named after him!" said the officer as he gave his son a pinch and gave Bill a knowing wink.

"Hey, Bill. Do you mind if I put up a poster for the Police Benevolent Association? Our big charity golf tournament is next month, and we need to raise some money."

"No, not at all," Bill answered while he continued stuffing groceries into burlap bags. "I hope you can find room between the other posters. The high school is doing 'The Sound of Music' next week, so you'll have some competition until then."

"Has Mattie's Uncle Henry stopped by?" asked Officer O'Brien as he searched for a prime spot in the store's front window.

"I haven't seen him yet, but he promised me that he would stop in after we opened. I'm looking forward to seeing him and hearing what he has to say about the store," Bill said with a twinkle in his eye and a smile that seem to cover his entire face, the kind of smile that shows through the eyes of wisdom and grace.

Eric Demaree

CHAPTER TEN

The Lessons

I wrote this book as a tribute to all the Masterful Merchants that I have had the pleasure of working with over the past 40 years. I have tried to apply the lessons they taught me to more than just running a business or retail store. I've tried to apply them to my life.

Through the simplicity of the message in this book, I hope everyone feels as I do. To be truly successful in business and life, you have to value People first. Above all else, taking care of People is the most important thing all of us can do.

Retail is tough. Real tough. Many small independent retailers have struggled. The ones that are no longer around blame the economy or the impact that major national chains have had on their business. As true as these realities are, there are still many highly successful independent retailers. They are the ones that understand how to effectively compete in today's marketplace. They understand the importance of operating on all seven cylinders, all the time. In simple terms, they live by the seven principles.

My question for everyone is this...If executing the seven **P's** sounds so easy, then why don't more retailers do it consistently?

When I ask most independent retailers that question, the same answers come up. "I don't have the time. How can you expect me to get employees to act like owners? I'd love to execute the seven **P**'s, but I do not have the money."

Some answers are very valid. Some are excuses that go on and on. Not to sound too harsh, but some excuses are a way for retailers to avoid the "painful self-examination" required to fix their problems. A lot of successful, entrepreneurial spirited retailers let their experience make them fail. They find it much harder to embrace and try new ideas, so they continue doing the same old comfortable things.

Everyone in retail realizes that today's customer demands everything that the seven principles require and more. Just merely executing the seven **P**'s may be what is required to be in the game. To be successful, every retailer must unlock the key to delivering a highly personalized and pleasantly memorable customer experience.

The seven principles are no more than a foundation which every retailer must ingrain into their daily habits in order to truly build a customer first culture. A customer first culture must be so deeply rooted in every employee that **"the behavior towards the customer must always be for the customer."**

Doing what's right for every customer, even the ones that don't treat you so nicely, is the first key to executing the seven principles. The order in which each word is presented really does not matter. It's the message that the seven **P**'s delivers.

>Caring **People**
>>Who **Position** and **Present Products**
>>>**Promoted** and **Priced** in a safe, secure and saleable manner
>>>>Fulfill the **Promises** made to every customer

In simple terms, that's what helps create a **Profitable** business.

The Masterful Merchant

PART TWO

WORLD-CLASS COMPANIES ARE BEATING THEIR COMPETITION THROUGH A CUSTOMER FIRST CULTURE

World-Class Companies are Beating Their Competition Through a Customer First Culture

The information contained within this section and within this publication only provides guidance on how to build a caring culture. This guidance is solely based on my own observations of what I believe are best practices effectively employed by successful companies. It should not be taken as anything more than guidance, and it is not meant to be a representation of laws or legal issues that must be adhered to when hiring employees for your business.

You should always seek legal counsel to address many exceptions to hiring practices and special situations that apply from state to state and in particular employment circumstances that may pertain to your company. I have included in this section what I believe all companies need to do to create, nurture and grow a caring culture that believes in and follows the seven principles.

Eric Demaree

PRINCIPLE No. 1
PEOPLE – THE RIGHT PEOPLE

Under the first principle, PEOPLE,
the topics covered include:

1
Steps you can take to create or re-create a clearly defined Mission Statement that will move your company closer to achieving its Vision

2
A process to follow so you can build specific job descriptions that clearly state the skill sets, behavior style and personality that you feel will attract the right people

3
An Interview Guide to organize your questions and record notes so you can compare different candidates' responses to the same questions

4
A list of suggested questions to use during interviews to assess if a candidate's behavior and personality will be a cultural fit

5
An interview evaluation sheet to ensure that you are executing the hiring process consistently and efficiently with every candidate

1

Steps you can take to create or recreate a clearly defined Mission Statement that will move your company closer to achieving it's Vision

If you want to build a culture within your company that truly cares about the customer, then your employees (I'll refer to employees as "People" from here on) have to understand and passionately believe in your Vision Statement and in your Mission Statement and have to live by the company's Core Values. They also have to believe that the company truly cares about them as individuals. The best companies have leaders who continuously keep their finger on the pulse of their employees to see if they are truly committed, through their words and actions, to helping the company achieve its Vision.

Ask these questions: Do my People behave in a manner that is supportive of the company values? Do they passionately believe in the Mission of the company and show it through their actions? Do they believe that they can have a significant impact on helping the company achieve its Vision? Do they feel appreciated for the work they do? Do they feel properly rewarded for the work they do? Do they understand their job descriptions and the performance expectations that are required of them by the company? Do they feel and act empowered to do things right and to do the right things, even when no one is looking?

If you answered yes to all of the above, then **skip this section**.

If you did not answer yes, then I hope by reading through this section you will have a starting point to create within your company a culture driven by dedicated, caring People.

You must clearly define who you are and what you want in order to hire the **Right** People. Ask yourself questions like: "Who are we as a company? Why are we here? What is our mission or purpose? What makes us special? What is it that what makes us different from any company that does the same thing we do?"

I find it helpful whenever going through this exercise to think about what I call "iconic companies." Choose companies that evoke in you and in customers indelible images of who they are and what they do. Sometimes a simple tag line will get your mind swirling and lead you to a more clear definition of the image you are as a company and may help answer some of the questions listed above.

Here are some examples:

Avis: "We try harder"
FedEx: "When it absolutely, positively has to be there overnight"
Burger King: "Have it Your Way"
Allstate: "You're In Good Hands"
Budweiser: "The king of beers"
Disneyland: "The happiest place on earth"
General Electric: "We bring good things to life"
Wal-Mart: "Save money...live better"
Subway: "Eat fresh"

Each tag line is a short statement of what each company does and what they offer to the customer. Employees (People) know that their companies have a promise to fulfill with every customer (their Mission). Wal-Mart's promise of "Save money...live better" is carried through in their Mission to "*help people save money so they can live better.*"

What is it that your company does that you could distill down into one simple tag line? If you have a Mission Statement, does it support a one line simple promise? Starting with a simple tag line will sometimes help lead to a Mission Statement that will help all your People see and believe in the Vision for your company.

Using Disney as an example, their tag line is simple, "The Happiest Place on Earth." Their Mission Statement is clear:

"To be one of the world's leading producers and providers of entertainment and information. Using our portfolio of brands to differentiate our content, services and consumer products, we seek to develop the most creative, innovative and profitable entertainment experiences and related products in the world."

Disney employees (People) are called "Cast Members," and when you ask them what it is they do, they say, "We Make People Happy."

I don't know about you, but I'm pretty happy when I'm at Disney. In fact, I feel pretty happy when I think about Disney. In fact, I spend a lot of money whenever I go to Disney, and they seem to be doing pretty well when it comes to generating profit.

Another company that makes me feel pretty happy is Southwest Airlines. In their best selling book, *"Lead with LUV,"* the past President of Southwest, Colleen Barrett, and her co-author, Ken Blanchard, talk about how Southwest achieved unprecedented growth and profitability in an industry that has been fraught with bankrupt airlines and has one of the worst reputations for providing customer service.

When Southwest hires People, Colleen will tell you that they *"hire for attitude and train for skills."* They take care of their People first, so that their People can take care of their customers. It is a culture carried through from the top of the organization. Gary Kelly, Southwest CEO says, "Our people are our single greatest strength and most enduring long term competitive advantage."

In their corporate headquarters in Dallas, there is an inscription engraved on a glass elevator wall in the lobby that tells the world what Southwest Airlines is all about:

"The People of Southwest Airlines are the Creators of What We Have Become and of What we will be. Our people Transformed an Idea into a Legend.

That Legend Will Continue to Grow Only So Long as It Is Nourished By Our People's Indomitable Spirit, Boundless Energy, Immense Goodwill, and Burning Desire to Excel.

Our Thanks and Our Love to the People of Southwest Airlines for Creating a Marvelous Family and a Wondrous Airline!"

If I visited your company, what would I see? Would I see People who have an *"Indomitable Spirit, Boundless Energy, Immense Goodwill, and Burning Desire to Excel?"* Would I see a *"Marvelous Family and a Wondrous Company?"* Would I hear your People ever use the word "LOVE?"

Do you feel your People are your "single greatest strength and most enduring long-term competitive advantage?" Do your People believe you feel that way about them?

Amy Klaris and Greg Ellis lead the Customer Experience Practice for the international consulting firm, Kurt Salmon. Their studies show that *"winning retailers will create connections with consumers that go beyond just transactions."* These "connections" happen across a broad array of channels that influence the customer, but they start with People. From the company founders and leaders down to the mailroom. From the People who operate and support your store to the People who staff your phones and your call centers. Connections to customers are made by anyone who is a touchpoint with your customers.

In the book *The New Rules of Retail*, co-authors Robin Lewis of The Robin Report and Michael Dart of Kurt Salmon's assert that *"going forward, retailers must create emotional ties to consumers."* Only People, caring People, can create emotional ties to consumers.

Eric Demaree

Emotional ties come through product, product presentation, product promotions, product positioning, product promises, product pricing, and people (7 Principles) who can, according to best selling author, Rick Barrera, "*Over Promise and Over Deliver.*" Do the People in your company create an emotional tie to your customers?

2. Build specific job descriptions that clearly state the skill sets and behavior personalities that you feel will attract the right people

As basic as it sounds, a properly designed, thorough job description is a key starting point in attracting the right People to your company. Your job description should look better than any competing company. It should be professional and reflect what you feel represents what is at the core of your company.

In addition to the job title and summary description within the body of your job description, you should have clearly defined parameters around the following:

Desired business experience - Education requirements - Objectives - Accountabilities - Competencies - Personal Behaviors - Personal Contributions - Work Schedule - Compensation and Benefits

The following definitions will help you think through and formally define each aspect of the job you are looking to fill as you build your job description.

Desired Business Experience

Business experience is defined by experience in the work force and also experience in a particular industry and potentially in a similar position. You must consider all facets. As an example, does your company want 5 years experience in the work force and 5 years of relevant industry experience or does industry experience matter?

To determine the desired level of work experience for any position, there are many questions to consider:

1. Are the desired experience requirements consistent with the job's responsibilities?
2. Can an employee perform the job with less experience? Why or why not?
3. Are you being objective or subjective when determining experience requirements?
4. Are you compromising on experience requirements to fill the job quickly?
5. Are your requirements realistic?
6. Are your requirements in accordance with all employment laws and regulations?

Narrow down exactly what you are looking for in an employee's experience and understand exactly why you are establishing specific parameters. That way you will be better able to focus your candidate search and better able to make a smart hiring decision.

Education Requirements

Consider the following questions:

1. What education is necessary to successfully perform this job?
2. Why is this education necessary?
3. Can this position be performed by someone with less education?
4. Are the education requirements consistent with other positions inside the company and the industry?
5. Are you being objective or subjective with these requirements?
6. Are your requirements realistic?
7. Are your requirements in accordance with employment laws and regulations?

These questions serve to clarify the position and the requirements. It is easy to set too low or too high a level of standards and therefore possibly miss the perfect candidate. By being as specific as you can, you'll be more efficient at eliminating candidates that do not fit your profile and more effective in finding those candidates that do.

Objectives

What do you want your new employee to do for your company? What are your goals for this position? Once you establish realistic goals that you want to see a person achieve in the position you are filling, then it will be easier for someone to achieve them.

Accountabilities

How will the employee be held accountable for failures and rewarded for successes? Who will determine failures and successes? Who will the position report to and what other relationship will the candidate have with supervisors?

The following questions can help determine reporting relationships and accountability measures:

1. What position or positions does this job report to?

2. Where does this position appear on the department's organization chart?

3. What employees or positions report directly to this job?

4. What is the relationship between this position and other positions within the company and within the department?

5. Will position and/or department be rewarded for accomplishing objectives?

6. If yes, then how will they be rewarded?

7. If no, then how will successes be acknowledged?

8. How will position be held accountable for not meeting set objectives?

Competencies

Questions related to competencies will help determine if a candidate has the desired attributes or skill sets that you want in an employee. They can include knowledge, skills (relationship skills, technical skills, selling skills), attitudes, and actions (decisiveness, urgency, prioritization, organization).

For any position, you would want to determine the candidate's effectiveness on the job by evaluating their ability to:

> *Achieve Results - Communicate Effectively - Demonstrate if they are Dependable - Make Effective Decisions - Plan and Organize - Problem Solve and Show Good Judgment - Be Productive - Collaborate - Work within a Team - Take Responsibility*

This is not a comprehensive list of competency behaviors. You should develop your own list that fits the attributes and behaviors a candidate must have for each specific position within your company. For example, if you want your employee to make effective decisions, how will you go about determining if they are capable?

Personal Behaviors

As important as the questions are to determine competencies, are the questions that determine the personal behaviors you feel are necessary for the position. Your questions should center on evaluating a candidate's behavior and personality in the following areas:

> *Ability to build Trust – Honesty – Level of Interpersonal Skills – Attitude (both positive and negative) – Ability to recognize the Achievements and Contributions of others – Ability to constructively resolve Conflicts – Shows Respect for others (verbal and non-verbal) – Supports Diversity – Understands Related Issues – Understands Alternative Perspectives*

Again, this is not a comprehensive list. There are literally thousands of websites and companies that can provide list of behavioral questions to ask during an interview.

Personal Contributions

You should also ask specific questions where a candidate can show how she/he contributed to the success of any previous organization including: leadership and initiative – creativity and innovation – customer orientation – their commitment to self-improvement, learning and development – their ability to adapt and be flexible – evidence of their commitment to teamwork – do they have vision and what did they do to bring their vision to fruition?

When you're hiring at the management level there are additional behavior considerations including how the candidate performs in:

Evaluating Employees – Enabling and Empowering Employees – Encouraging Teamwork – Recognizing Group Achievement – Identifying and Supporting Opportunities for Employees to Develop and Advance – Leading Change – Achieving Results

There is a long list of behaviors to consider when you're searching for the right employee(s). Many of the behaviors are already defined in the basic job description that you have developed without even thinking about it in specifics. Once you list the behaviors that are desired, why they're desired, and how you plan on evaluating whether or not a candidate possesses those behaviors, then the last thing you need to do is ask the questions in a very structured way during every interview with every candidate.

Work Schedule

Most work policies are presumably already established. If it is a new position then decide the work schedule, including the times of day that you want the employees to start, the time the work day ends and how many hours a week you expect them to be there. Also determine in advance which days, if any, are paid holidays, vacation days, personal days, etc. If alternative work schedules are available, like telecommuting or working four 10-hour days, then determine that as well. It is always advisable to have a detailed employee handbook, so that nothing is left to interpretation, for example, Compensation and Benefits.

You should already have a company wide benefits package and policy in place. However, if there are any exceptions, for example, room to negotiate salary requirements, extra vacation, or other exceptions to the company benefits packages, then those decisions need to be made in the beginning.

JOB DESCRIPTION

Here is an example of a job description you might modify for a Sales Professional. With any Job Description, try to keep it to no more than 2 pages. Once written, a great way to get it posted to multiple sites is through *http://www.ziprecruiter.com/*

POSITION: Sales Professional **DATE: mm/dd/yyyy**
REPORTS TO: Sales Manager **CARES FOR: The Customer**

Sales Professional

(Company Name) Sales Professionals are Sales Caretakers. They take care of every customer and sell products and value-added services that deliver to each customer a highly personal and memorable shopping experience.

Responsibilities
Selling to Customers
- Learns, embraces, and uses the tools as required by the company, including:

    o Customer-centric Selling Skills
    o Product Knowledge
    o Operating Systems
    o Store's Policies
    o Competitive Shops
    o CRM and Lead Management Systems
    o Financial Performance Reporting Metrics
    o All Safety Standards

- Develops Product Expertise by completing schedule of on-going Product Knowledge (PK) courses as required by the company

- Learns all operating systems and procedures to service the customer, including, but not limited to, computer order entry and product look up, credit applications, managing multiple customer transactions, taking customer deposits, coordinating and managing projects, etc.

- Understands other job responsibilities within the company that contribute to and support the customer shopping experience

- Visits online websites of industry associations and manufacturers to stay current with all industry trends and to gather information.

- Establishes with Sales Manager pre-determined sales goals and accountability measurements

- Measures and tracks key individual sales metrics

- Completes all training programs in a timeframe required by the company
- Analyzes and shops all competition as required by the company

Caring For Customers
- Over promises and over delivers on all orders and services
- Owns the entire customer experience from start to finish
- Follows up in a timely fashion on any and all customer issues
- Resolves customer complaints immediately
- Keeps customer profiles up to date in CRM and lead systems
- Organizes a constant contact process to facilitate on-going customer communication and direct marketing
- Builds and markets added value services/products to existing customers
- Builds and maintains repeat and referral customers through Personalized e-mails, handwritten thank you cards, special personalized invitations, freebies when appropriate

Caring For the Store
- Helps keep store GRAND OPENING READY everyday
- Maintains store neatness and cleanliness to promote a professional selling environment

Desired Work Experience

Education Requirements

Minimum Skills Required

3

Create and Follow an Interview Guide to organize your questions and record notes so you can compare different candidate's responses to the same questions

---

T he resources available on-line today are endless. You can research multiple sites for free or go to sites where you can pay for guides that you can customize to fit your requirements. You can also have candidate's answer formal questions online. Here is one site that is worth visiting: *http://www.selectpro.net/*

4. Develop specific questions to use during interviews to assess a candidate's behavior, personality, and potential cultural fit

For decades, many companies have used behavioral interviewing techniques to get a better feel for whether or not a prospective candidate can operate within their culture and fulfill the requirements of the position(s) they are looking to fill. Employers want to do everything possible to determine a candidate's potential for success and to avoid the costly mistake of hiring the wrong person, so many will use behavioral interview techniques to evaluate a candidate's experiences and behaviors.

The beauty of the internet is that you can Google just about anything and get help or answers to any questions you may have on any subject. There are endless resources that can provide lists of behavioral questions to ask. For example, when Accenture hires, they look for the following:

"There are five very specific things we look for with our entry-level hires. The first is GPA. Secondly, we look for people who have an interest in and understanding of our work. We look for students who have participated in outside activities. We really like to see people who have led those outside activities. The fourth thing would be someone who actually worked while in school. To us this is all about well-roundedness, the ability to multi-task and balance. Finally, we look for people who display very good professional presence.

"For experienced hires we typically look for individuals who have a broad range of functional and technical skill areas and industry specialization." Stacey Jones, Accenture spokeswoman

In an interview, Accenture will base their behavioral questions around some of the characteristics that they feel are critical for a candidate to be successful within their organization. These include: teamwork – professionalism – evidence that the candidate is a self-starter – willingness to travel – willingness to pursue advanced learning – has the ability to perform critical thinking.

Accenture, as well as many other employers, will structure very specific questions to get from the candidate very detailed responses, so they can determine if the candidate possesses the desired personality and behavioral traits necessary for the job.

Here is a partial list of desired behaviors you should review to determine how to ask the right behavioral questions. **Cultural fit is one of the most critical requirements** if you want to increase your chances of finding and hiring the Right People.

Desired Behaviors:

Shows and demonstrates that they are a servant leader – genuinely likes people – adaptability – communication oral – communication written – communication-non verbal (i.e. body language, facial expressions) - ability to control (emotions, passion, vocally) - analytical ability (financial, situational, conflict) – attention to detail – critical thinking ability (decisiveness, best choice, research, details, thoroughness) - ability to effectively delegate and follow up/follow through - proof that she/he can develop people - energy – entrepreneurial spirit – willingness to take risks – empowerment (both giving and excepting) – insightful – visionary – strategic – big picture - knows how to talk – how to ask the right questions – how to get to the right audiences - shows flexibility – initiative – innovative – judgment (good judgment) – leadership - ability to effectively listen - ability to motivate – influence - has practical skills – negotiating

Eric Demaree

– organizational management – prioritizing – time management – planning – presentation (written and verbal) – has sales ability – persuasiveness – no fear – persistent – tenacious - loves collaboration – teamwork – puts others out front - is respected by industry & other professionals - shows exceptional knowledge – proficiencies - shows uncompromising work standards – highly ethical – high integrity – treats work as a career not just a job.

You can build your own list of questions, but make sure they ask for a specific example that reveals their behavior. They can start out with: "Tell about a time when you..." or "Describe a situation that you found..." Read Hiring for Attitude by Mark Murphy, CEO of Leadership IQ. http://www.leadershipiq.com/books/hiring-for-attitude/

You should use a rating system to evaluate what you feel are the most important behavior criteria during the interview. Here are several sources:

http://www.quintcareers.com/sample_behavioral.html
http://humanresources.about.com/od/interviewing/a/interview_odd.htm

There are a boat load of other professional services available. There are psychological testing services, assessment companies, profiling services, etc. etc. etc. (I do not have enough etc's.). A lot are free, but the best are ones you pay for. All are worth exploring. Nothing is more important than finding, hiring and keeping the right People. Try the following:

www.discoveryreport.com
www.zeroriskhr.com
http://www.q4solutions.com/
http://www.super-solutions.com/onlinepersonalitytests.asp#axzz1aUrOZ9Jg
http://www.personalityinsights.com

5 Create an interview evaluation sheet to ensure that you are executing the hiring process consistently and efficiently and properly evaluating every candidate

You can pull any type of interview evaluation sheet off multiple websites, but you should take the time to develop your own and prioritize the criteria that are the most important behavioral skills you need for each position.

Here is a simple format that uses a 4 to 1 rating, where 4 is high and 1 is low:

CANDIDATE: (name)
INTERVIEW DATE: mm/dd/yyyy
POSITION: (job title)
INTERVIEWED BY: (name)

1. Personal appearance (first impression, grooming, body language, facial expression, vocal inflection, expressiveness). Rating: _____

2. Attitude (outlook, courtesy, responsiveness, respectful/politeness, mood). Rating: _____

3. Personality and maturity (friendliness, self-confidence, rapport, realistic, sense of humor). Rating: _____

4. Communication skills (verbal, written, non-verbal, participation in interview, persuasiveness, clarity, conciseness). Rating: _____

5. Mental alertness and cognitive abilities (logic, response to questions, inquiring mind, potential for growth). Rating: ___
6. Motivation and drive (initiative, achievement-oriented, energy level). Rating: _____
7. Interest (in company, breadth and general interest, knowledge of profession). Rating: _____
8. Leadership ability (desire to organize and direct, willingness to accept responsibility). Rating: _____
9. Overall evaluation. Rating: _____
10. Would you like to have the applicant work for/with you? Yes/No.
11. Would you recommend the applicant for employment? Yes/No.

Here is another approach you could use to formalize your own assessment:

How does the applicant's initial appearance impress you?
- Excellent first impression
- Good impression
- Satisfactory
- Somewhat unfavorable
- Poor

How do the applicant's manners impress you?
- Pleasing
- Agreeable
- Adequate
- Awkward, ill-at-ease
- Offensive

Is the applicant effective in communicating his or her thinking?
- Excellent choice of words
- Good choice of words
- Sometimes at a loss for words
- Limited vocabulary
- Ineffective

What degree of determination does the applicant seem to possess?
- Strong determination
- Good determination
- Some determination
- Easily discouraged
- Gives up easily

Does the applicant give evidence of initiative?
- Strikes out for himself/herself
- Needs little direction
- Some originality
- Wants to be directed
- Needs to be directed

How hard do you believe the applicant will work?
- Consistently hard worker
- Will work systematically
- Satisfactory
- Tends to take things easy
- May loaf on the job

What degree of enthusiasm does the applicant seem to possess?
- Exceptional
- Above average
- Average
- Some
- Very poor

Has the applicant shown evidence of leadership ability?
- Constantly
- Frequently
- Occasionally
- Seldom/Never

What potential does this applicant possess?
- Exceptional
- Very good
- Average
- Very little
- Poor

Would you want the applicant to represent you or the company at a meeting?
- At any meeting, large or small
- An asset to any organization
- Will be very effective
- Will be moderately effective
- At small affairs only
- Will antagonize most people

I recommend this applicant for employment in the above-named position:
- Strongly agree
- Agree
- Disagree
- Strongly disagree

One last note... look deep inside your company and give yourself a little "self quiz."

What do you want people to feel when they think about your company? Do your people feel happy? Do they feel valued? Do they genuinely want to care for your customers? Do your people respect you? Do they like you? Do you feel your customers like your company? Do your customers like you? Or better yet...do your customers **love** you?

It may sound a little 'Goofy' (sorry for the Disney reference again, couldn't help myself), but research conducted by Kurt Salmon, the International Consulting firm, showed that consumers are twice as likely to shop at stores they love compared to stores they like. What separates stores that we "**like**" versus stores that we "**love**" is the quality of the People we encounter in each.

Capturing and keeping loyal customers today, more than ever, requires a strict discipline to executing flawlessly the 7 Principles described in this book. But above everything else, without dedicated, sincere, genuine, caring, passionate and compassionate People, customers will see or perceive little or no difference between your company and every competitor.

As more and more companies move toward "sameness" in the eyes of the customer, the major chains win. Customers will shop wherever the closest store is located. There will be no "loyalty" to any company, and for most, why should there be? A lot of companies are not willing to invest in finding, training, rewarding and retaining the Right People. The only way to overcome "sameness" is through People...People who deliver a highly personal, memorable shopping experience...every time...to everyone!

PART THREE

UNDERSTANDING THE MODEL OF HUMAN BEHAVIOR

By Robert A. Rohm, Ph.D.

PEOPLE 101

7 Principles, whether in a small 'mom and pop' corner store or a company the size of the block, are vital in building and securing a successful venture! From little Lisa's Lemonade Stand on Saturday morning in the neighborhood to Amazon Inc., the first principle, **People,** is the foundation for the other six. The dreamer, creator, inventor, designer, architect, engineer, partner, employee, sales manager and marketer are all people. In the final analysis, it ends where it all began; it's all about Principle 1: **People!**

Part 3 of this book is about how individuals are wired. **The DISC Model of Human Behavior** will be your guide into what you need to know about the first Principle in order to successfully complete any joint venture. For over 2000 years, the study of people has mystified all of us. We are very curious about our own value and purpose, and, when we collaborate with others, we wonder why we work well with some people but can barely tolerate others. If we are to accomplish something together, whether it be raising a child or creating a worldwide retail market for our own product, our success and happiness depend on how well we understand and communicate with others. Part 3 of this book will help you understand how to interact with others in a way that strengthens the whole team and, thus, the whole project.

How important is it to understand personality styles...to recognize how someone is 'wired' for personal greatness...to know how personality styles are suited for leading or for following...to predict patterns of responses necessary in a specific job? Basically, how important is it that we all succeed in any endeavor when the vision can only be accomplished by the 'sum' of us, not 'some' of us?

We think it is very important!

Moreover, this book will show you how disagreements and healthy conflict can be the fuel for creativity and innovation when the team understands and respects the different personalities at the table. Without this understanding, the cogs in the wheel become clogged with emotional pettiness and ideas will slow to a halt; a visionary's nightmare. Part 3 will give you that 'understanding' which has been proven to keep the wheels moving, especially in conflict. And all you need to begin is the answers to two questions...

First Question:
Am I more *Outgoing* or am I more *Reserved*?

Second Question:
Am I more *Task-oriented* or am I more *People-oriented*?

UNDERSTANDING HUMAN BEHAVIOR

Over twenty-four hundred years ago, keen observers of human nature began to notice predictable patterns of behavior. In time, these observations led to developing the **DISC Model of Human Behavior** to describe these patterns. Understanding these patterns in human behavior will help you improve your understanding of both yourself and others. The charts in this section illustrate the model and serve as a ready reference for you as you read this book.

Each person has an internal motor that drives them. This motor is either fast-paced, which makes some people more **OUTGOING**, or, it is slower-paced, which makes other people more **RESERVED**. The illustration to the right shows this difference graphically. The shading of the arrows from lighter to darker indicates varying intensities of these drives. Close to the midline shows less intensity in the motor activity, therefore light shading. Toward the outer edge shows more intensity in the motor activity, therefore darker shading. You may be extremely OUTGOING or extremely RESERVED. Or, you may be only moderately OUTGOING or moderately RESERVED.

OUTGOING

RESERVED

Just as each person has a motor which drives them, everyone also has an internal compass that draws them toward either tasks or people. Some people are more **TASK-ORIENTED** - drawn toward tasks. Other people are more **PEOPLE-ORIENTED** - drawn toward people. The illustration shows this difference graphically.

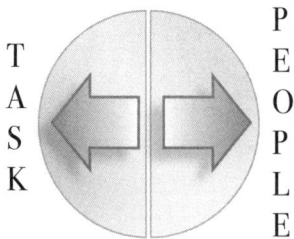

The shading of the arrows from lighter to darker indicates varying intensities of this compass drive. Close to the midline shows less intensity in this compass drive, therefore light shading. Toward the outer edge shows more intensity in this compass drive, therefore darker shading. You may be extremely TASK-ORIENTED or extremely PEOPLE-ORIENTED. Or, you may be only moderately TASK-ORIENTED or moderately PEOPLE-ORIENTED.

When you put together both the Motor and Compass Activity drawings, you see the Model of Human Behavior illustrated on the next page.

In the diagram on the next page, notice that each **DISC** type has a group of descriptive words that relate to behavioral characteristics of that personality style. These descriptive words show traits or tendencies that describe each type. The main characteristic trait for each type is used as the representative word for that type: Dominant, Inspiring, Supportive, and Cautious.

Notice that people who are: Quadrant

Outgoing and Task-oriented are...	DOMINANT	D
Outgoing and People-oriented are..	INSPIRING	I
Reserved and People-oriented are...	SUPPORTIVE	S
Reserved and Task-oriented are...	CAUTIOUS	C

Here are some shortcuts you can use in discussing the different types of people:

the DOMINANT	type is also known as High **D**
the INSPIRING	type is also known as High **I**
the SUPPORTIVE	type is also known as High **S**
the CAUTIOUS	type is also known as High **C**

This model can help you understand people by describing four main, or primary personality styles. However, each individual person will display some of all four personality styles. This blend of styles within each person is called a style blend. Each person's style blend will have more of some traits and less of others. The types that are strongest in a style blend are called high styles. The types that are less prevalent in a style blend are called low styles.

Outgoing – Task-Oriented	Outgoing – People-Oriented
Dominant Direct Demanding Decisive Determined Doer	Inspiring Influencing Impressionable Interested in people Interactive Impressive
Percentage of population: 10–15%	Percentage of population: 25–30%
Percentage of population: 20–25%	Percentage of population: 30–35%
Cautious Calculating Competent Conscientious Contemplative Careful	Supportive Stable Steady Sweet Status Quo Shy
Reserved – Task-Oriented	Reserved – People-Oriented

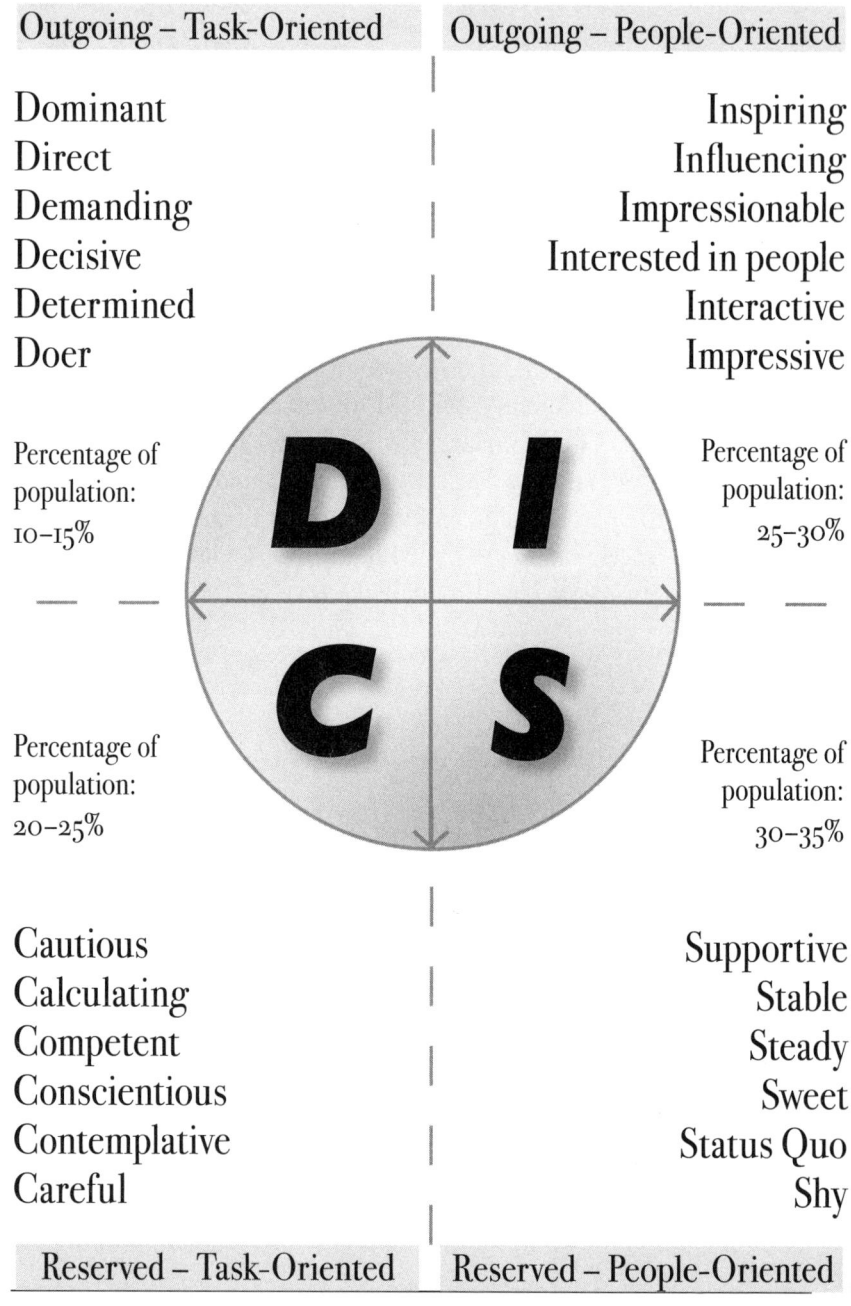

Dominant Type   Inspiring Type

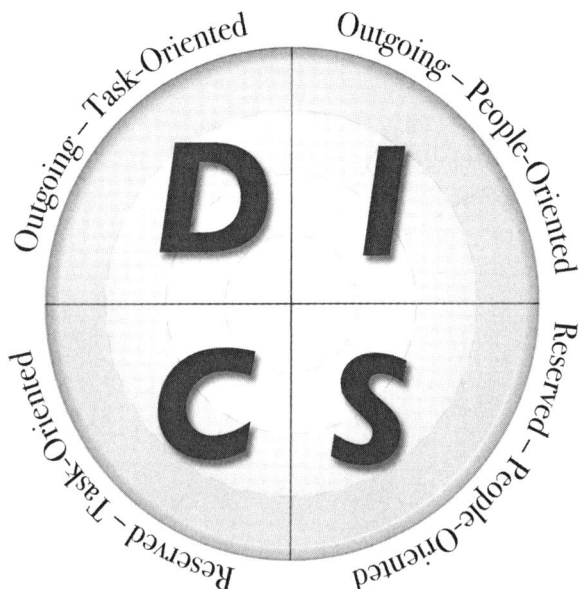

Cautious Type   Supportive Type

Remember:
Everyone is a unique blend
of these four parts,
with a higher or lower
intensity of each D I S C
Personality Style.
This is simply your starting point as you
learn and grow in all four areas of life!

Also remember that most people are predominantly strong in one or sometimes two different areas. Everyone is "wired" differently. You may only relate to one of the traits or you may relate to all four of them. And, in addition to that, you may feel that you really do not understand one of the types at all. This is perfectly normal and natural. We generally have some of all four personality types within us, to a greater or lesser degree. Most often we have one or two high types, and one or two low types. The payoff for learning about your low types is invaluable, because this is the place where you can learn and grow in your own personal life about areas you might misunderstand. It is also a great opportunity to learn about someone close to you.

Personality Style Blends

Only a very small percentage of people have a personality style blend that is just one high DISC type. Most people (about 80%) have two high DISC types and two low DISC types in their style blend. This means that one DISC type may be highest in your style blend, but you probably also have a secondary DISC type which is also high. This secondary type supports and influences the predominant type in your style blend. For example:

A person who has the **I** type highest and **S** as a secondary high type, would be an **I/S** style blend.

A person who has the **I** type highest and **D** as a secondary high type, would be an **I/D** style blend.

While both of the people in the example above are High **I** types, the difference in their secondary traits would make them very different people.

It is less common, but not highly unusual, to have a third high type in a style blend (i.e. **I/SC** or **I/SD**). Approximately 15% of people have three high DISC types and one low DISC type in their style blend.

This blending of personality styles in each person helps to account for the large variability among people even though there are only four primary types described by this model.

When you read the term "High **D**", "High **I**", "High **S**", "High **C**" - that simply means a person is strong or predominant in that trait.

Likewise, when you read the term "Low **D**", "Low **I**", "Low **S**", "Low **C**" - that simply means a person is weaker or less predominant in those corresponding traits.

As you looked at the style descriptive words for each type, you may have felt that you could relate to some of the words in several, or even all, of the DISC types. The styles where most of the words describe you are probably your high styles. The styles where only one or two words describe you are probably your low styles. That is okay. This is just a reflection of your unique style blend.

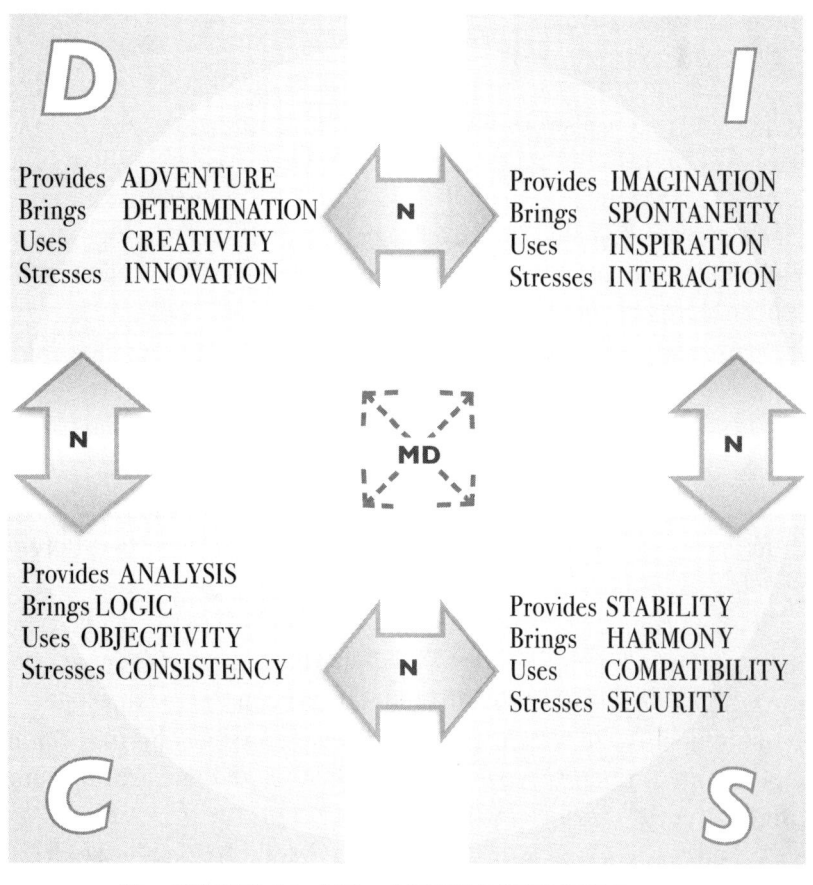

N = NATURAL; MD = MORE DIFFICULT

Personality Combinations

Whenever two people interact, their personality style blends come together to form a *combination*. This combination is unique to each interaction of people. Adding a third person to the mix forms a different combination. A forth person would form still another combination, and so on. The real power in understanding personality information lies in developing the ability to recognize these different combinations and to adapt yourself to new situations as they constantly arise.

If we can understand each other and adapt to each other better, we can enjoy one another more and increase our productivity at the same time. The book, *Who Do You Think You Are... Anyway?*, explains many of the factors which work for and against harmony in all kinds of relationships. Here we will specifically explore how the combination of your style with the styles of your clients will affect your business relationship. We will also offer tips on how to make your interaction with your clients more convincing based on the styles of the people involved.

The great news is that you can learn to relate better with virtually everyone! Your ability to understand and apply personality information to build stronger relationships is known as your Personality Quotient (**PQ**). Learning experts say that people can do little to change their Intelligence Quotient (IQ). They say that IQ is fairly well fixed at birth. However, unlike your IQ, you can develop your **PQ**. So, you can have greater success with anyone you meet, whatever their style.

These personality insights can help you increase your effectiveness both in your business and in your personal interactions! Use these personality insights to gain a broader perspective on how you represent yourself and your business. Your PQ, not your IQ, qualifies you to effectively interact with others.

Four Steps to Raising your PQ

1. Understand the Model of Human Behavior.
2. Understand yourself by understanding your personality style.
3. Understand another person by understanding their personality style.
4. Adapt your style to have better relationships.

As you continue to read part 3, you will see other people's actions and reactions from a new perspective. You will begin to understand them better than ever before. You may even begin to think about how they see you, too. Have fun exploring how you can apply these concepts in your life and business.

We spend years in school developing our intelligence to effectively use our minds. Developing our unique personality to effectively use our behavior is just as vital to successful living. Your Intelligence Quotient, or IQ, measures your intelligence. Your Personality Quotient, or **PQ**, refers to your ability to understand yourself and others for effective communication and teamwork. Studies have shown that technical skill, beginning with intelligence and developed through education and experience, accounts for only 15% of success in the workplace. The other 85% of workplace success comes from people skills! These skills are developed through learning better ways to behave and interact. In reading these pages, you are taking the first vital step to understanding your Personality Quotient. As you answer the question, "What's your PQ?" you can work toward more productive interaction and behavior. After all...

"If I understand you, and you understand me, doesn't it make sense that we can work more effectively together?"

General Insights

You will probably identify best with the traits in one of the type descriptions in the following pages. Because you are a blend of all four styles, you may also see parts of your personality style in one or two of the other type descriptions. You are likely to identify least with the remaining type descriptions. This is perfectly normal.

We suggest that you initially focus your attention on developing a growth plan based on your primary personality style. As you learn to use the strengths and compensate for the blind spots in your primary style, you can then focus your attention on other aspects of your unique style blend.

It is possible to form a fairly accurate picture of your basic personality style blend by simply reading the following sections and looking for statements and perspectives that fit your natural perspective. For a more complete picture of your unique style blend, we recommend that you get a custom-prepared Personality assessment. This report will identify, with great accuracy, how your blend operates in life and in business. It will reveal your natural strengths and also highlight the struggles you may face in adapting your style. The report includes specific suggestions for creating an action plan to help you achieve greater success.

The High D Traits

As a two year old, this person's first sentence was probably "I do it MYSELF!" They continue to say that for the rest of their lives. People with High **D** traits approach everything they do with energy, focus, and tenacity.

The exclamation point represents the power of this style! They are demanding, first of themselves, and then also of others. We can admire their boldness and willingness to tackle difficult tasks. **D**s are direct, saying what they mean and meaning what they say. They echo the words of Napoleon, "Circumstances? I make circumstances!" **D**s are determined to make things happen! They bring this strength to the business, where they not only drive themselves, but can also motivate others to achieve.

We say that **D**s are dogmatic because they are so confident. They believe that if the dream is big enough, the facts don't count! They may not recognize that they need help missing the pitfalls that are sure to come as they deal with people, but they are diligent, hard workers. Their dynamic personality type can be the driving force behind a great organization!

Can be described as:	Dominant, Direct, Demanding, Decisive, Determined, Doer
Characterizing Symbol:	Exclamation point – You are emphatic in everything!
Characterizing Color:	Green – for go
Outlook on life:	You probably like to lead or be in charge.
Focus:	Get the job done – just do it! Overcome opposition and achieve your goals! Winners never quit and quitters never win!
Ideal environment:	Upbeat, fast, powerful

People with High **D** traits:

- Set clear goals and persist to accomplish them
- Do not get disturbed by the word NO. To them, NO means ASK AGAIN LATER
- See opportunities, not problems
- Like competition and respond positively to sales promotions
- Have tremendous energy
- Have the drive to achieve Top Producer status
- Have innovative ideas
- Enjoy the independence of their position
- Make decisions quickly and then work to make the decisions happen
- Like negotiating
- Will work long hours
- Like to solve problems

D Types don't like...

- INDECISION
- SLOW PEOPLE
- TALKERS WHO DON'T PRODUCE
- POOR PERFORMANCE
- DETAILED ACTIVITIES
- TAKING ORDERS

UNDER CONTROL	BLIND SPOTS
COURAGEOUS	RECKLESS
QUICK TO RESPOND	RUDE
GOAL-ORIENTED	IMPATIENT
RESULTS - ORIENTED	PUSHY
DELIBERATE	DICTATORIAL
SELF-CONFIDENT	CONCEITED
DIRECT	OFFENSIVE
SELF - RELIANT	ARROGANT
STRAIGHTFORWARD	ABRASIVE
COMPETITIVE	RUTHLESS

COURAGEOUS:

The **D** will gladly take on the business challenge of making the calls, driving the miles and meeting the obstacles, no matter what they might be. Pushed out of control, they can become RECKLESS by doing or saying things to accomplish their goals that may hurt the people involved.

QUICK TO RESPOND:

Ask a **D** a question and they may answer you before you finish the question. They are quick to respond directly and to-the-point. Out of control, they may come across as RUDE. Because the High **D** is determined to get results, small talk seems pointless, and they will often miss the sensitivity to people it can afford. Others may find their quickness to respond overbearing and rude when they never mean to give that impression.

GOAL-ORIENTED:

They not only set goals – they achieve them! In business, once a **D** makes up their mind to do something, they drive for the goal. If the goal seems more difficult than they expected or than they deem worthy, they can become IMPATIENT. Leadership is a natural part of their style and business goals, so they may become impatient to assume leadership roles before they are offered or earned.

RESULTS-ORIENTED:

The task orientation of a **D** will keep them very focused on getting the results they desire. And results are important! It is difficult to measure intent, desire, or excitement, but anyone can measure results! A High **D** needs to remember that others may not share this drive, and if they become PUSHY, they will not like the results. They must understand that "winning at any price" may cost them with people in ways they will later regret.

DELIBERATE:

Ds do things very deliberately and must have a purpose for doing anything. They enjoy strategy and planning every step they will take in building their business. They are sure that their plan will work. In their determination, they can quickly become DICTATORIAL, if they force people to fit into their plan. People may withdraw from working with them, and the High **D** will not understand why.

SELF-CONFIDENT:

The High **D** believes they can overcome any barrier or solve any problem. This confidence sustains them as they build their business. If success comes too easily or too quickly, it may allow the High **D** to become CONCEITED, and people will quietly walk away because they feel the High D cares only for themselves.

DIRECT:

You will always know exactly where you stand with a **D**! They say what they mean, and mean what they say. As they deal with people, they will be direct to address a problem instead of holding a grudge. When a difficult or complicated situation needs to be handled with sensitivity, their directness can feel OFFENSIVE and may alienate the people involved.

SELF - RELIANT:

Ds take care of themselves and will rely first on themselves to get the results they want. They encourage others by their example and in words to believe that they can also be successful. Out of control, they become ARROGANT, thinking that they can accomplish their dreams alone. They may forget that they need many different people to build a business.

STRAIGHTFORWARD:

What you see is what you get with a High **D**. They clearly tell you about the situation and what they want to accomplish. Because the goal is so important to them, they discount their own feelings in a situation and can easily become ABRASIVE to people when they just as easily discount the feelings of others. They expect people to choose to feel how they have chosen to feel. They need to learn to be considerate of others, realize that others feel differently, and respect those feelings. The High **D** will benefit from the better relationships that this respect will build for them.

COMPETITIVE:

A **D** loves to make anything a game that they can win! They see competition as a natural motivation to do better. In business, their competitive spirit will spur them on. If they become RUTHLESS in order to win, they will hurt many people, including themselves. They must learn the truth that all of us are better than just one of us!

The conversation of a High **D** tends to be bottomline and to the point. They make flat statements and challenge the comments of others. They really do not need the facts someone uses to support their comments – they want to know instead that the speaker really believes what he or she says and will stand behind those words with actions. They do not mean to offend others and are surprised if someone feels affronted by their straightforward approach. If you can understand that this is an issue of style, you can more easily accept and forgive whatever the High **D** does that goes against your style.

How to be the best High D possible

The High **D** personality has determination. If this is you, you have the drive, the focus, and the persistence to accomplish any task or challenge. In fact, you may view conquering challenges as fun. It can drive you to succeed. Your need to have a challenge is a huge asset.

High **Ds** NEED:

- Challenges
- Control
- Choices

These three needs make sales attractive to people with High **D** traits. People with High **D** traits often want to be their own boss. They want to have the control to make decisions and to have choices so that they control their destiny. They are generally self-motivated and task-oriented so they enjoy being the lone wolf while running the roads. They tend to view every potential sale as a challenge to meet with determination. They are often comfortable using a direct, matter-of-fact approach. They usually exhibit great energy, and they value productivity.

Issues that often cause stress for High **Ds**:

- Being taken advantage of
- Losing control
- Being disrespected
- A slow pace
- Talk that does not lead to action

Under pressure High Ds may react with (blind spots):

- Impatience
- Sarcasm
- Pushing for results (forcing a close)
- Intense physical expression
- Loud vocal tones

People with High D traits will get better RESULTS when they:

- Become accountable to someone or allow a mentor to critique their performance
- Slow down, cultivate active listening skills, and learn to speak in softer voice tones so that they avoid coming across as pushy or overbearing
- Remember to smile and take the time to socialize with the client

The High I Traits

The theme song for High Is could be "Don't worry, be happy." They love to have fun and to interact with other people.

What could we give the High I that would be better than a big red star? Maybe two?! This symbol recognizes their type with that red star! Life for this type is six fun Saturdays in a week! They always find ways to make work into play. We can admire this ability to brighten almost any situation. They live by the words of comic Joe E. Lewis: "*You only live once – but if you work it right, once is enough!*"

The High I experiences everything and loves to express what they feel in that experience! They are carefree and outgoing because they are naturally trusting, even to the point of sincere gullibility. The High I may exhibit more confidence than ability because they tend to be very optimistic and disinterested in details. They are engulfed by each experience, so they can easily make life an emotional roller coaster for everyone. They can feel higher than a kite one minute and lower than a skunk the next. They make friends easily because they certainly feel that a stranger is just a friend they have not met! More reserved types may feel overpowered by them and shy away from their open, emotional advance, but we all love the fun we have with them! Their fun comes right into the business with them!

Being without a definite plan is not a problem for a friendly, fun-loving, and impressionable I, who is happy just talking with people. They need help learning to listen because each thing they hear seems to remind them of something else they need to say! Their ability to meet and make new friends can boost their business, but they will always need to remember to take time in their fun to get down to some serious business.

Can be described as:	Inspiring, Influencing, Impressionable, Interactive, Impressive, Involved
Characterizing Symbol: ★	Star – Give them a RED STAR! They need to be noticed and recognized.
Characterizing Color:	Red – it says "Notice me!"
Outlook on life:	They like to persuade others to their way of thinking.
Focus:	I am for you! Let's have some fun! If we all pull in the same direction, our success will never end!
Ideal environment:	Fun, friendly, exciting

People with High I traits:

- Like to meet new people. They make cold calls warm within a few moments
- Project a likable attitude
- Enjoy interacting with people, they speak to others with ease
- Show enthusiasm
- Inspire customers to buy
- Have tremendous energy
- Will work hard because they want to please and impress superiors
- Work well in an informal or unstructured environment
- Quickly adapt to changes, they have great flexibility
- Add fun and excitement to the work place
- Encourage others
- Exude optimism

I Types don't like...

- BEING IGNORED
- BEING ISOLATED
- BEING RIDICULED
- REPETITIVE TASKS
- DETAIL WORK
- LONG-TERM PROJECTS

UNDER CONTROL	BLIND SPOTS
OPTIMISTIC	UNREALISTIC
PERSUASIVE	MANIPULATIVE
EXCITED	EMOTIONAL
COMMUNICATIVE	GOSSIPY
SPONTANEOUS	IMPULSIVE
OUTGOING	UNFOCUSED
FERVENT	EXCITABLE
INVOLVED	DIRECTIONLESS
IMAGINATIVE	DAYDREAMING
WARM/FRIENDLY	PURPOSELESS

OPTIMISTIC:

They are cheerleaders for their group, always looking for someone to cheer on to victory in the business! They can really encourage the group through some difficult times. Pushed to an extreme, they can be UNREALISTIC as their optimism loses credibility when they overlook facts which may be essential to arriving at correct conclusions or even misjudge the complexity of a problem they currently face.

PERSUASIVE:

They are engaging talkers and enjoy telling stories about important people they may have met. It is simply amazing how many people they know! They also have a talent for weaving yarns, drawing from many examples they have heard from many sources into their discussions about the business. But, if their stories bend the facts too far, others will feel they are MANIPULATIVE, simply trying to get people to do what benefits the High I. This manipulation can cause huge resentment and seriously damage relationships.

EXCITED:

They are so excited, and their excitement is infectious! They attract and energize people. They make work so much fun that achieving great goals seems possible, even worth trying to reach! If they face disapproval or public embarrassment because in their excitement they promise what they will not deliver, they can become EMOTIONAL and explode with an unexpected attack. They can become more consistent (and therefore more credible) when they are accountable to someone to help them remember to do what they said they would do when they were excited enough to make a commitment.

COMMUNICATIVE:

They do not hesitate to say almost anything to anyone! How easily the High I can start a conversation or explain their point of view! Most people find it easy to listen to them and enjoy being around them. People are attracted to them for encouragement and coaching. Because they like to talk and share what they know and whom they know, they can be GOSSIPY, sharing private information without meaning to hurt.

This hurt may easily divide and damage people. A High **I** can learn to recognize privileged information to protect the privilege of knowing that person.

SPONTANEOUS:
Life would be much less fun without the spontaneity of the High **I**. They are always ready to enter a door of opportunity that can lead to unexpected results in their business. Out of control, their spontaneous nature can become IMPULSIVE and burn up their energy without producing business results.

OUTGOING:
The outgoing **I** type will go to a party and know everyone there before they leave. This is great in prospecting for building their business! Trying to be involved in too many opportunities can make them UNFOCUSED.

FERVENT:
When they believe in their business, they really believe! They will be so convinced that they are fervent about getting the word out and getting others involved. Sometimes they can seem so EXCITABLE that people won't believe the opportunity they describe is real or attainable.

INVOLVED:
The High **I** loves to be in the middle of whatever is happening! Because they so enjoy activity, they may be DIRECTIONLESS in their participation and miss opportunities to promote their business.

IMAGINATIVE:
What ideas this **I** type can create! Their imagination can conceive what most of us would not dare to dream. Such dreams can be a wonderful motivator in this business. However, imagination can replace reality when DAYDREAMING takes over with ideas that have no purpose or use in achieving the dream.

WARM/FRIENDLY:

Everyone feels that the High **I** is their friend because of the warm, friendly feeling they receive from the I. Because business is built on relationships, their business will prosper. Unfortunately, the High **I** can be superficially friendly and become PURPOSELESS in getting the results for business success.

Conversations with **I** types can be lengthy and free ranging, because one thing just leads to another! They tend to make emotional rather than rational statements and often will think out loud. They can jump quickly from one idea to another and leave others questioning their conclusions. They tend to talk things out rather than think things through. Other styles must recognize that when the High **I** makes a pronouncement, they are verbally testing ideas. Then other styles can give them room to alter their opinions. If you can understand that this is an issue of style, you can more easily accept and forgive whatever the High **I** does that goes against your style.

You may have heard business leaders say that their business really got going when it moved from their head to their heart. The High **I** style usually starts with their heart! They may struggle getting the business out of their heart and into their hands and eventually to their feet! Their talk and their feelings about their business may be genuine, but translating their feelings into appropriate action may be more difficult for them. Understanding the need to make their commitment match their inspiration is key to their success in business.

How to be the best High I possible

The High I personality is a team player! If this is you, you likely live to inspire and influence anyone who gets within five feet of you. You probably love people and feel comfortable speaking with almost anyone.

High Is NEED:

- Recognition
- Approval
- Popularity

Gaining the acceptance, love, and admiration of the multitudes (the more the merrier) fuels many people with High I traits. They often enjoy the limelight that sales presentations place upon them. They not only want to make the sale, they usually want the client to love them. They often mix their sales pitches with many humorous anecdotes. In their effort to keep the spotlight on themselves, they might dominate the conversation. At times, they can talk the ears off of a corn stalk! Very little stimulates them more than public recognition for their sales accomplishments. Their driving need for popularity and social acceptance might create an equally strong fear of social rejection. In the face of rejection, High Is tend to react emotionally.

Issues that often cause stress for High Is:

- Rejection
- Public embarrassment
- Loss of social standing and recognition
- Large quantities of detailed information
- Highly structured environments

Under pressure High Is may react with (blind spots):

- Talking
- Laughing
- Emotion
- Diverting attention
- Joking

People with High I traits will have more FUN when they:

- Get organized and avoid misplacing paperwork and contact information
- Focus on their goals and the task at hand to become a great finisher
- End their day on a positive note, listen to a motivational CD, or read from a positive book. Avoid allowing one unsuccessful call or frustrating day to ruin their emotional outlook and productivity.

The High S Traits

People with High **S** traits tend to have a quiet, laid back exterior. They generally like to work at a steady pace, and they usually like to know how things will turn out before they begin.

This symbol shows a plus and minus sign to represent the ability of the High **S** to do more or less what they need to do to give their support for continued harmony among people. The High **S** is people-oriented, but reserved. While a High **I** tends to be a "Here I am!" kind of person, an **S** is a "Here we are!" type. They love their home and family, and seek a steady and stable environment for everyone to share.

Natural timidity can be a struggle for the High **S** because they do not want others to feel that they are pushy. The High **S** may need to remember how much they appreciated the person who showed them their first home, so that they will feel comfortable showing properties to others.

You may have heard successful real estate couples say that one spouse, "gets people to look at houses" and the other spouse is able to make people "feel at home." Often they mean that the outgoing one is good at stirring up enthusiasm in the new prospect, while the other is good at long-term relationship issues and can smooth over offenses and disappointments along the way. The latter is the strength of the High **S** in the business. It is easy for some to overlook or undervalue these gentle skills, but someone with a warm, quiet demeanor becomes a trusted friend everywhere.

For these slower-paced people, this axiom is essential: Give yourself time to succeed. There are many highly successful people who have a High **S** personality style, proving that "if you can build a relationship, you can build a business."

Can be described as:	Supportive, Stable, Steady, Sweet(nice/kind), Status quo, Shy
Characterizing Symbol: $\pm$	Plus or minus sign – Either way is okay with them... They feel that harmony is what we need.
Characterizing Color:	Blue – calm and serene like the clear, blue sky
Outlook on life:	They like to provide support to help complete the job.
Focus:	All for one and one for all! If we all work together we make a great team. All of us are better than one of us.
Ideal environment:	Predictable, stable, harmonious

People with High S traits:

- Listen well
- Make people feel comfortable and at ease
- Build strong relationships with their customers
- Create trusting relationships so that customers return
- Follow leadership well
- Finish what they start, once they get moving
- Avoid conflict and will keep the work place peaceful
- Like to work in a team environment; often willing to assist other sales people
- They give great customer service because they aim to please
- Have an easy-going approach
- Are dependable
- Feel comfortable doing repetitive tasks – follow through, etc.

S Types don't like...

- INSENSITIVITY
- TO BE YELLED AT
- MISUNDERSTANDINGS
- SARCASM
- SURPRISES
- BEING PUSHED

UNDER CONTROL	BLIND SPOTS
RELAXED	LACKING INITIATIVE
RELIABLE	DEPENDENT
COOPERATIVE	A "SUCKER"
STABLE	INDECISIVE
GOOD LISTENER	UNCOMMUNICATIVE
SINGLE-MINDED	INFLEXIBLE
STEADFAST	RESISTANT TO CHANGE
SOFTHEARTED	EASILY MANIPULATED
SYSTEMATIC	SLOW
AMIABLE	RESENTFUL

RELAXED...

Their easygoing style will bring comfort to those around them. They don't like to be pushed and can be indecisive when you ask them for an opinion. They try to give the answer that they think you want to hear. In their hesitation, they can LACK INITIATIVE and let opportunities pass by them.

RELIABLE:

At every meeting, they are reliable to be there. They will always do what they say they will do for you. Because they need affirmation, they may become DEPENDENT on others and slow down the process.

COOPERATIVE:

When the High **S** cares for you, they are very cooperative to help anywhere you may need them. To help you, they may sacrifice their own needs and can be A "SUCKER" and let others take advantage of their good nature.

STABLE:

The High **S** brings stability to a business because they appreciate the success of a proven routine. They are comfortable with things that stay the same and will remind the other styles to think again before making a change. They can be INDECISIVE about choosing change even when it will make their business grow.

GOOD LISTENER:

Their associates and clients will appreciate what a great listener the High **S** is. They will give many hours supporting and caring for others. Even though they do so much listening they can be UNCOMMUNICATIVE about how they feel, thinking that their situations are not as bad as other's so there is no need to talk about themselves. They can be left carrying their own burdens and the burdens of the rest of the world.

SINGLE-MINDED:

Once a business system or method has been accepted, they will be very true and faithful to the system; other ideas or methods may be presented but they will reject them. They can be INFLEXIBLE about trying new concepts that could really benefit them.

STEADFAST:

You may be ready to skip to the next chapter of this book, but the steadfast **S** is comfortable at this point and will find insights that you may miss! They will be firm in using tried and proven methods in their business; even though times may change, they may be RESISTANT TO CHANGE that must occur for further business growth.

SOFTHEARTED:

In a cold-hearted world, the High **S** will bring a tenderness and care that will really help others in the business. Unfortunately, through this kindness they can be EASILY MANIPULATED to serve the selfish intentions of others.

SYSTEMATIC:

The High **S** will do their work the same way over and over again. While being systematic ensures that they will get predictable results, others can be frustrated when the **S** is so concerned about following the system that they are too SLOW in getting things done.

AMIABLE:

The High **S** is so friendly and kind that amiable really describes them! If someone needs their help, they will happily help them. Even if they continue to help, they may feel they are being taken advantage of and may inwardly become RESENTFUL and gradually withdraw their support. Raising their **PQ** to do what is best for them too will help them prevent this resentment.

In their reluctance to be seen as pushy or assertive, they often keep their opinions and feelings to themselves unless they are asked or really feel hurt and angry. Do not assume that if they have an issue with you, they will confront it. Generally, they "stuff" their feelings because they want to avoid conflict. When you directly ask them about their feelings, they often diminish the intensity of their response because they can feel intimidated easily. Rather than confronting you or addressing their feelings, they may quietly continue doing things their own way.

How to be the best High S possible

The High S personality is a loyal team member! If this is you, your ability to persist and finish what you start makes you the follow-up and follow-through expert. You almost certainly excel at maintaining existing clients because you make time to get to know them, support their needs, and follow-through on your promises.

High Ss NEED:

- Appreciation
- Security
- Assurance

Little pleases people with High S traits more than bonding with the people around them to accomplish a common goal. Warm-hearted, pleasant, and natural TEAM players, they often work behind the scenes to make things happen. When a problem occurs, High S sales people generally find a way to take care of the customer. They often do this personally. They might try to keep the peace regardless of the personal cost to them.

Issues that often cause stress for High Ss:

- Conflict
- Confrontation
- Loss of security
- Sudden change
- Multiple high priorities with short deadlines

Under pressure High Ss may react with (blind spots):

- Procrastination
- Indecision
- Compromise
- Silence
- Withdrawal

People with High S traits will get more COOPERATION when they:

- Project confidence in their service or company
- Practice assertive communication skills to manage customer expectations – clearly define delivery dates, fees for extra services, etc.
- Recognize that a direct question or a "no" from a customer is not a personal attack

The High C Traits

People with High **C** traits can achieve success because of their relentless and methodical approach. They usually like to "plan their work and work their plan."

This symbol shows a question mark to represent how the High **C** asks many questions. They love to bring order out of chaos by understanding a system and knowing how to make everything fit within it. They prize consistent quality and excellence. This preference carries over into their business, where they find it easier to complete correct order forms than to deal with people.

If you have a question about a listing or details of a house, ask a High **C**! They carefully study all the details and other issues that affect their business. Their conscientious attention to the facts builds quality and excellence in any organization. They like to document everything they do, to know the in-depth reason behind the in-depth reason. **C** types can be so precise that their handwritten paperwork sometimes looks as if it has been typed. Their concentrated effort to be completely correct may immobilize them from taking action on an issue. They do not like carelessness in others and do not tolerate mistakes in themselves. Their need for correctness can make others feel that they are cool or aloof. Making an effort to convey warmth will help the High **C** be more successful in business.

They like to ask questions and verify answers. At times, others may feel their questions sound like, "What about this? What about that? What about the other thing? What about...?" Always another question! The High **C** does not understand how this could be a problem, since they still need to validate quality, detailed answers. They tend to analyze almost everything, and enjoy finding and correcting mistakes. People may feel that **C**s are picky or fault-finding, but they are simply convinced that anything worth doing is worth doing well. When they do reach a conclusion, they tend to draft firm and defined plans, and they will resist making unnecessary changes without solid reasoning. They will work the system to achieve business success.

The Masterful Merchant

Can be described as:	Cautious, Calculating, Competent, Conscientious, Contemplative, Careful
Characterizing Symbol: ?	Question mark – They want to know the "why" behind everything.
Characterizing Color:	Yellow – it stands for Caution
Outlook on life:	They like consistent quality and excellence.
Focus:	Anything worth doing is worth doing correctly. They want to provide quality goods and services through careful and conscientious work.
Ideal environment:	Structured, accurate, High quality

People with High C traits:

- Know their product(s) and service(s)
- Make clear and logical presentations
- Often anticipate and rehearse answers to the most likely questions their clients might ask
- Have very high standards for themselves
- Act with great integrity and honesty
- Finish whatever they start
- Seek perfection personally and professionally
- Carefully plan their work and work their plan. They will not entertain distractions
- Methodically work their territory
- Maintain objectivity
- Often analyze and pursue the most efficient approach to time and territory management
- Value loyalty

C Types don't like...

- BEING CRITICIZED
- MISTAKES
- SUDDEN CHANGES
- SHODDY WORK
- UNPREPAREDNESS
- UNNECESSARY INTERRUPTIONS

UNDER CONTROL	BLIND SPOTS
ORDERLY	COMPULSIVE
LOGICAL	CRITICAL
INTENSE	UNSOCIABLE
CURIOUS	NOSEY
TEACHABLE	EASILY OFFENDED
CAUTIOUS	FEARFUL
CORRECT	RIGID
QUESTIONING	DOUBTFUL
CONSCIENTIOUS	WORRISOME
PRECISE	PICKY

ORDERLY:
Their business will be very organized and structured, which will keep their system running smoothly. As their intense focus increases, they can become so concerned about every detail that they become COMPULSIVE about little issues that are not important. This frustrates people who work with them and may cause people to give up trying to satisfy the expectations of the High **C**.

LOGICAL:
The High **C** must make logical sense of everything. They tend to ignore their feelings in favor of logical facts. They will carefully and completely think through every area of their business. In their unending quest for perfection, others may feel that they are just CRITICAL of everything and everybody. Operating in their blind spot, their critical nature may drive people away from them.

INTENSE:
When they are focused on business, nothing can pull them away. The world can totally pass them by while they are reading all the detailed information. As their intensity magnifies, they can become UNSOCIABLE, concentrating on details that seem more important to them than people are.

CURIOUS:
The High **C** is insatiably curious. They just want the facts–all the facts! They have just one more question that needs to be answered before any conclusion can be drawn. This desire for the facts tends to make them NOSEY about others' personal lives. The High **C** may ignore their own feelings, but if they want to enjoy people, they must learn to respect the feelings of others.

TEACHABLE:
Their quest for knowledge and quality answers keeps the High **C** very teachable. They always want to learn new procedures and understand what others are doing. When the suggestions take issue with the correctness of the way they are already conducting their business, they can be EASILY OFFENDED and defensive against all

suggestions. They need to be convinced that their old way was right, but the new way is better.

CAUTIOUS:

They are cautious, never wanting to make a mistake. Their cautious nature can predict and prevent many costly mistakes in their business. They are constantly checking themselves and may become so FEARFUL of breaking the rules or not getting it right that they can become immobilized.

CORRECT:

The High C could say, "Do it right or don't do it at all!" They want to be correct, so they will follow their Plan step-by-step. This intense need to follow their plan in any area of their business can cause them to be too RIGID, not allowing for other possibilities to achieve their goals.

QUESTIONING:

The High C is questioning. They ask the questions that must be asked and others have missed. If an answer depends heavily upon emotion, or really has no definite answer, they may become DOUBTFUL of everything and everybody and lose their focus.

CONSCIENTIOUS:

They will carefully cover every detail of their business. Every piece of paperwork will be completed, copied and filed on time. As their business expands, they will have a tendency to be WORRISOME over all the details that must be handled correctly.

PRECISE:

All the numbers and facts given to you by a High C will most likely be correct. You can be sure that they are right about their business. Since they want to be so precise, they can easily become PICKY about others and the way they achieve their goals. They may need to show others why they feel the need to be so precise, or they can be perceived as a critic.

The Masterful Merchant

Channing Pollock once said, *"A critic is a legless man who teaches running."* It is possible for Cs to be seen as this kind of a critic. However, with a small adjustment to their approach, another **C** word that could suit them as well would be "a coach." Because they are able to view circumstances less emotionally, they often can provide a more objective solution to a difficult situation.

How to be the best High C possible

The High **C** personality seeks excellence! If this is you, you set high standards for yourself, and you are likely to study all of the details about whatever product or service you sell. Your methodical approach to handling your territory and your detailed preparation for every sales presentation makes you a valuable asset to your sales team. You probably strive for excellence and perfection in everything you do.

High Cs NEED:

- Quality answers
- Value
- Excellence

As highly logical thinkers, people with High **C** traits carefully evaluate and explore all options to develop a procedure or plan to anticipate and prevent mistakes. They generally prepare well for every presentation. They may even have typed notes and refer to accurate graphs and research. They work hard to "keep all of their ducks in a row." They excel at organizing information, developing flow charts, and following rules.

Issues that often cause stress for High Cs:

- Unknown or unclear expectations
- Illogical actions
- Disorganization
- Inconsistency
- Violating principles

Under pressure High Cs may react with (blind spots):

- Criticism
- Pessimism
- Asking pointed questions
- Judgment
- Correcting others

People with High C traits will achieve EXCELLENCE when they:

- Recognize that "good enough" really is good enough so that they take action rather than over analyzing a situation.
- Learn how to give a brief overview of a presentation. Giving too many facts and details can make a sales presentation difficult to follow for other personality styles.
- Loosen-up and smile. Remember – people don't care how much you know until they know how much you care. A smile will create a better connection with more people.

BUILDING RAPPORT
Bridging the Broken Bonds of Trust

Once you reach someone, you need to quickly overcome their skepticism. They may be naturally skeptical people, but more likely they have learned skepticism from past experiences with other people in the past. So, how do you do overcome skepticism? We suggest that you attempt to come across in a way that invites your prospect to like you so that you can build rapport with them.

As a professional, you may have already heard that you need to build rapport with your clients. Just to make sure that we work from the same understanding of this concept, we will begin with some definitions and observations.

The American Heritage Dictionary defines rapport as:

- relationship, especially one of mutual trust or emotional affinity.

Effective business people know how to establish rapport with their prospects and clients. They understand this general rule:

> *We tend to connect with and like people who are similar to us. Unfortunately not everyone is like us!*

Ultimately you want to reach the rapport stage in relationship with your clients. However, you will not likely reach that level of connection in the first conversation. During the conversation, target a friendly connection so that you have the opportunity to meet with your prospective client. Remember, most decisions – especially buying decisions – are first emotion based and then supported by logic. If you connect with your prospective client, you will book more meetings. When you book more meetings, you make more business. So, develop the skill of connecting with people.

Notice that we use the word "skill" to describe this ability. Every personality style has both strengths that help them build connections and blind spots that limit their ability to connect with others. Regardless of your personality style, you can learn the skill of connecting with people. Once you make a connection, you can then work on building rapport.

The process of building rapport varies with the person, but we do notice some patterns. We can look at the process from two different perspectives: task-oriented and people-oriented. The process of building rapport follows the general flow shown below.

The Rapport Building Process

Task-oriented individuals tend to move through these steps as they go from the initial connection to a state of rapport.

Connect => Trust => Relationship => Rapport

People-oriented individuals tend to follow the same steps, but in a different order.

Connect => Relationship => Trust => Rapport

First, notice that the rapport process always begins with a connection. At the connection stage, your client starts to think (if they are task-oriented) or feel (if they are people-oriented) that they like you. This thought or feeling will most likely start because they see a part of themselves in you. Remember the general rule:

> *We tend to connect with and like people who are similar to us. Unfortunately not everyone is like us!*

The next steps in the process depend on your prospective client's primary drive.

Building Rapport with Task-Oriented Individuals

For most task-oriented individuals, after making a connection, their next thought in the process of building rapport focuses on trust. In looking at you, they often ask themselves these questions:

- "Can I trust this person to do what they promise?"
- "Can I trust this person's information?"
- "Can I trust that this person is honest and truthful?"
- "Can I trust that this person will respect my time?"
- "Can I trust that this person will be logical?"

Once they decide that they can trust you, they are more likely to take the initial connection deeper to a relationship stage. From the relationship stage, they may be willing to move to the deeper level of rapport.

Building Rapport with People-Oriented Individuals

For most people-oriented individuals, after making a connection, their next step in the rapport-building process will come from how they feel about you. In deciding if they can move with you to a friendly relationship level, they may ask themselves questions like:

- "Does this person care about me?"
- "Does this person genuinely like me?"
- "Do I feel good about this person?"
- "How does this person treat other people?"
- "Will this person listen to me?"

Once they decide that they feel good about you, they then observe how the relationship develops (how you interact with them and others) to decide if they can trust you. When they reach the trust stage, they may be willing to move to the deeper level of rapport.

The rapport-building process has many implications that lie outside the scope of this book. For now, we just want to gain some initial insights into what really happens in this process and to recognize that the process changes from person to person depending on their blend of task and people traits.

For the purposes of this book, we want to introduce the concept of the rapport-building process and give you some background information to use. The rapport-building process has greater significance in face-to-face meetings than it does in any brief telephone conversation. We offer the information here so that you have a starting point for understanding the different perspectives people often take with regard to building rapport.

We think that you should notice the flow so that you can better understand your client's perspective. For now, though, we want to turn your attention to the first step of the CALL method and the first step in building rapport – CONNECT with the person.

Making a Connection

You probably only have a few seconds of interaction during your initial encounter. So, what do you do? You cannot possibly assess the exact style blend of the person in such a short time. So, we recommend that you listen for, and respond to, what you hear in the other person's voice. You do this in two steps.

Connection Step 1: Listen for vocal pace and volume

If they speak quickly and loudly, they are probably more outgoing. If they speak slowly and softly, they are probably more reserved. If their pace and volume matches your natural pace and volume, great. You will probably connect fairly well. If you notice that you speak at a different pace and volume from them, just adjust to match them.

To develop a connection quickly, practice matching the mood, pitch, speed and volume of your prospective client. When people hear themselves in your voice, they tend to connect with you or like you.

Connection Step 2: Decide if they are task or people oriented

Once you have made a guess about whether they are more outgoing or reserved, you then try to decide if they are more task-oriented (35% of the general population) or people-oriented (65% of the general population). This difference may not be immediately obvious. So, here is what we recommend: go with the odds. Initially assume that they are people-oriented and go for an emotional connection.

We recommend that you start with feeling words rather than thinking words because statistically most of your clients will tend to be more people-oriented than task-oriented. If your discussion continues for very long, you can listen for your prospective client's primary drive as well (as explained in this chapter).

Task-oriented people tend to say things like:

- "I think that..."
- "It seems to me that..."
- "How can I get more information about..."

People-oriented types tend to say things like:

- "I feel that..."
- "I'm not comfortable with..."
- "Who else can I speak to about..."

Many people ask the question, "What if they're task-oriented and you start the conversation with feeling words? Won't you miss the connection by assuming that they are people-oriented?" The short answer is: probably not.

If they are primarily task-oriented, they most likely have a strong people-oriented secondary trait. So, the odds of irritating them by attempting to connect on a feeling basis are low. In fact, if they have a very strong task nature, they might not even notice that you used a feeling, emotional approach. If you notice any disconnect at this point, just adjust your wording to a task/thinking basis. The point is this – put the odds in your favor to start the conversation and then adjust as necessary.

If you know the person you are talking to, by all means go with what you know about them and tailor your approach accordingly. The suggestion above assumes that you do not know the person. Just based on the odds (65% of people are people-oriented), you will be right more than you are wrong if you go for emotion first.

Putting it together, you will probably note the following information in all your conversations:

High - D clients – short, direct discussion with little small talk, probably decisive and quick to state an opinion

High - I clients – friendly, expressive conversation, probably willing to talk freely

High -S clients – friendly, soft conversation, probably listens more than they talk

High - C clients – short, precise, conversation, they may question you more than they state their position; likely to be cautious about making commitments

---

You just have to be aware of the differences and adjust your behaviors accordingly. Listen to your prospective client's word choice, vocal tones, and pace of speech then adjust yours to fit them.

This information will help you adjust your phone conversations and target your sales presentations to address your client's needs and concerns.

When you understand your style blend, and learn to identify and appreciate your client's style blend, you will communicate more effectively and connect with people more often.

The Simply Ask Technique

We say that to use this technique, you must Simply Ask. In other words, "Simply Ask" the person these two questions to help you identify the highest type in their personality style. Using this technique in countless presentations, prospecting, and just social situations, no one seems offended to answer two simple questions. We may have felt a little funny asking them, but no one seemed to mind answering them. Often, people will quickly answer the questions, then reply, "Why did you ask that?" This becomes an open invitation to engage in a meaningful conversation. Most people really appreciate an effort to better communicate with them. Open your doors of communication using this Simply Ask technique.

Simply ask these questions:

Question 1. Do you feel that you are more outgoing, or would you say you tend to be a little more reserved?

If a person responds by saying that they have some of both, you can reply, "That's true!" We all have some of both of these qualities. But, if you had to choose between the two, in which direction would you lean?"

Question 2. Do you think you are more task-oriented or do you feel more people-oriented?

Again, remind them that we may have both qualities, but you are asking which way they most often lean. Remember, you don't have to ask these questions one after the other like a machine gun, but gently ask them in the flow of normal conversation. Most people really enjoy talking about themselves and seem genuinely pleased when you show interest in them. If you are asked why, explain that you are interested in understanding them better, and that this helps you to begin to engage in that process.

The FORM Technique

We can remember the third technique for understanding a person's style from the acronym FORM. Using this FORM technique may take a little more time; we like to think of this as our advanced method since you must ask open-ended questions. Their answers may indicate the predominant type in their style. The FORM is:

F: FAMILY

Listen to their response about their spouse or children to DISCover if their description indicates that they are outgoing. Their conversation may reveal that they are more reserved instead. Also listen for an indication that they are more task-oriented or people-oriented.

For example:

"What do you enjoy most about your family?" – If they talk more about the characteristics of individuals they appreciate, they are probably more people-oriented. If they describe the roles and accomplishments of the individuals, they are probably more task-oriented.

Answer 1. "My husband is a dedicated doctor who really cares about his patients." This answer from the wife shows that she values who her husband is and that he cares for people. She is probably more people-oriented.

Answer 2. "My husband is a specialist who has a demanding practice." This answer would indicate that the wife values the work that her husband does and his expertise. She is probably more task-oriented.

Answer 3. "We love to go to different places and do new things together. We also enjoy great parties at home with many friends!" This answer would indicate that this person is probably outgoing.

Answer 4. "Our home is so peaceful and quiet. We enjoy reading wonderful books or working in our garden. We don't care for big groups or travel, except to visit family." This would probably indicate that they are more reserved.

Your skill will increase with practice as you understand that sometimes how the person describes what they enjoy is more important than what they actually say they enjoy. In a family, you are dealing with the personality styles of two or more people, so listen carefully to distinguish the difference between their own priorities and meeting the needs of others in the family.

O: OCCUPATION

What work occupies their time can tell you about their task and people skills, and whether they operate at a slower or faster pace.

For example:

"What do you enjoy most about your work?" – Listen closely to the answer to this question to determine if they are more outgoing or reserved, and more task- or people-oriented.

Answer 1. "I am one of the top salespeople for a major corporation. I have one of the largest territories with the top sales dollars." To handle this type of a position this individual must be outgoing just to get the results. Now you know the person must be in the outgoing half of the DISC circle.

Answer 2. "I am a chemical engineer for a small company. It's not very exciting, but I enjoy it. I just work in the lab most of the day." To do work in a lab all day would require a more reserved type person. You now can move your finger down into the reserved half of the DISC circle.

Answer 3. "I sell directly to the public. I really enjoy helping people. I also get to meet so many very interesting individuals!" This person seems to really enjoy people, which would indicate they are people-oriented.

Answer 4. "I like to say that I am a household engineer. I'm lucky if I manage to engineer a few minutes to do what I want to do in a day! Three children are a lot of work!" This person approaches caring for children as a task. You probably know that you are talking to a task-oriented individual.

Just by listening to a person talk about their occupation you should be able to determine whether a person is outgoing or reserved and task- or people-oriented.

R: RECREATION

What they do for relaxation and why they do it may indicate whether they are fast or slower-paced, and whether they enjoy tasks or people more. Look here for a common interest you may share to begin building a relationship.

For example:

"What do you like to do for recreation or as a hobby?" – Different types like different diversions for different reasons. Let's listen again to see if they may be outgoing or reserved and task- or people-oriented.

Answer 1."I just love to sit at home on the weekends and read a good book." This person sounds more reserved.

Answer 2. "I can hardly wait until the weekend to go out with my friends. We have a good time whatever we do!" From this simple answer you can safely identify a High **I**, who is outgoing and people-oriented.

Answer 3. "I compete on the tennis team in our neighborhood. When I don't have to work on an extra work project, I always have a project to finish at home. I like to coach my son's basketball team too." This person is probably outgoing and is more certainly task-oriented.

Answer 4. "Right now I am enjoying a fascinating study of my genealogy. I have traced my ancestors to Switzerland and northern Italy in the nineteenth century!" Only a reserved, task-oriented person would enjoy this kind of free time activity.

One question about recreation or hobbies can yield a wealth of personality information!

The last question explores what types of activities they enjoy to help identify what motivates them. Finding their passion will help you find their style and a bridge to communicate with them effectively.

M: MOTIVATOR

What is the reward a person needs for achievement? Is their passion the reward, recognition, achievement, appreciation, correctness, or challenge? Exactly what motivates them to excel?

For example:

"What do you find is your best motivator to help you really work at something? Do you have a dream for the future?" Listen again:

Answer 1. "I would really love to be able to give my children the support they need to complete their education." The word "support" may indicate a High **S** type, especially when their motivator seems to be supporting their family.

Answer 2. "I'm at my best when I go out and make things happen to get results!" Saying that he or she is best at getting results simply shouts a High **D** type!

Answer 3. "I really enjoy seeing things done correctly and carefully. I am most pleased with an excellent job delivered on time." See how quickly you key in to the words "correctly" and "carefully"? You may easily recognize this High **C** type.

Answer 4. "I love to get a party going and give people a good time. I dream about being on a stage, meeting my favorite star!" This person shouts High **I**, doesn't she?

The Masterful Merchant

Using the FORM technique can not only give you many indications about someone's personality style; it can also help you find a common interest for further conversation.

Almost anyone enjoys talking with someone who is genuinely interested in him or her. Sharing your own short stories about a common interest may open the door of opportunity to begin to build a relationship. Begin to recognize their personality perspective to better work with and communicate with them.

CLUES TO LOOK FOR

Following is our Clues and Ques chart. You can use this information from two directions: when you see these traits, tendencies and activities in an individual, you may more easily identify the high types in their style. From the opposite direction, when you already know an individual's style, you may predict and prepare for their possible actions and attitudes.

Since home is the best place to start, begin to notice the behavior of your spouse, your children, your friends.

Take a few minutes to explore the obvious indicators on the following page. Knowing the High types in your style, read the columns that may describe you. If you know your spouse or friend's style, read the columns that may describe them. Watching how someone lives every day will show you some of these obvious indicators. No matter what our personality style may be, each of us has a natural reaction to each of these areas. You may find some surprises hidden in this chart! You may, for the first time, begin to understand how your spouse shops from the Buying Methods! Have fun trying to find a friend who fits into each type!

Someone has said that agriculture is just like farming, except that farming is doing it. Until now, this DISC information has been an interesting theory. Now, you can begin to put it into practice! You want to have the tools to empower yourself to improve your life and business. Now is the time to try the Fourth Step to raising your PQ, Adapting Your Style to Have Better Relationships.

You can practice communicating more effectively as you recognize styles at a glance and adapt to their needs.

A story is told about a little boy who got into an argument with some kids twice his size. He drew a line in the dirt and dared them to cross it. Without hesitation, they accepted the challenge, whereupon the little guy smiled and said, "Now you're on my side!" That's the goal of applying this information: to bring us from opposing sides to the same side; to become a winning team.

Is this going to be an easy step for you? To start with this may feel like folding your hands a different way – remember how that felt? Talk with your family, friends and co-workers. Practice these concepts, and remember that you have been adapting all your life, but now you have the benefit of a pattern that makes sense! Start with the First Step, understanding the Model of Human Behavior. Then, move to the Second Step, understanding your own personality style. Then move to the Third Step, understanding another person and his or her personality style. Then move to the Fourth Step and adjust your own personality style. Before you know it, you will be connecting with other people in ways you could have never imagined! "The journey of a thousand miles begins with a single step...and a road map!"

Now that you know more, you will be able to do more!

On the next page you will see a helpful chart called *"Clues and Ques"* *to reading and understanding personality styles.*

This chart will give you further insights into the four personality styles.

Clues and Ques to reading and understanding personality styles

Obvious Indicators	D	I	S	C
Buying Method	Decides quickly; prefers new and practical	Decides impulsively, from feeling and appearance	Decides slowly; prefers the traditional	Decides cautiously; prefers the exceptional; likes value
Personal Decor	Large desk, awards, useful accessories	Flashy, trendy, with fun pictures	Family pictures, personal mementos	Aesthetically pleasing, unique, functional
Body Language	Big gestures; leans forward, advancing	Expressive, friendly posture; amusing	Gentle gestures; reassuring	Unemotional, controlled gestures; assessing
Organizational Method	Accessible, practical, not neat	Piles rather than files; disorganized	Systematic, traditional	Highly organized, personalized detailed system
Energizing Recharge	Competition; Physical activity	Interaction; Social activity	Retreat; Undirected activity	Solitude; Cognitive Activity
Speech Patterns	Directive tones, abrupt, interrupting always doing something	Talkative, varied tones, personal, easily distracted	Conversational, warm tones, friendly, prefers listening	Clarifying, monotone, logical, focused, emotionless

Understanding personality styles gives you an idea what to expect from a prospect in a conversation. You have also begun to understand how your personality style communicates. Take a few minutes to read the chart below. Read each column to understand the predictable patterns of each type. Then, perhaps you might like to read each row to see how DISC types can be different in so many ways! These clues should help you understand how your prospect may approach your conversation. Use it as a reference before contacting.

Pedictable Patterns	D	I	S	C
Wants to know:	What?	Who?	How?	Why?
Wants you to be	Direct	Excited	Sincere	Credible
Dreams of:	Accomplishments, money	Being a star	Security for family	Long-term profit
Processes information by asking:	What will work?	Is it fun?	Can you give me more time?	Is it logical?
Driven by:	Will	Feelings	Trust	Intellect
Key strength:	Firm	Fun	Friendly	Factual
Key struggle	To be friendly	To be factual	To be firm	To be fun
Secret to their success:	To be under authority	To be more credible	To be more decisive	To be more caring

It is also important to see what each personality style might look like when they get under pressure (as shown on the next page).

The DISC personality types under pressure:

- Impatience
- Sarcasm
- Pushing for results (forcing a close)
- Intense physical expression
- Loud vocal tones

TIP: (warning)
D Types do not take "No" for an answer. To them, "No" simply means, ask again in a different way.

- Talking
- Laughing
- Emotional noise
- Diverting attention
- Joking around
- Unpredictable

TIP: (warning)
I Types may be looking at you, but probably are not listening to you. Their mind is often somewhere else!

- Criticism
- Pessimism
- Asking pointed questions
- Judgmental
- Correcting others
- Defensive

TIP: (warning)
C Types process most information intellectually rather than emotionally. If you perceive something is wrong, simply remember, nothing may be wrong - they are just thinking or processing information.

- Procrastination
- Indecision
- Compromise
- Silence
- Withdrawal

TIP: (warning)
S Types often shut down emotionally and even physically when they feel the environment is filled with conflict. They prefer an atmosphere where there is peace and the feelings of others are considered.

Building Trust - What does communication **without** trust look like and produce?

Trust is a cornerstone for relating and communicating more effectively with others.

Without trust:

- Barriers and guards go up
- Lower performance
- Limited communication takes place
- Ideas and creativity stops
- Lower morale
- Increase in conflicts and misunderstanding
- People become indifferent
- Time and energy is wasted in conflicts

TOLERATE → AVOID → ELIMINATE

Attitudes that Create or Reflect a Poor Environment

Criticism	Uncommitted
Disengaged Involvement	Negative Assumptions
Indifference / Apathy	Unproductive
Resentment	Defiant Mindset
"Not My Responsibility" Mindset	Tension
Blame	Fear
No Accountability	Hurt Feelings
Low Morale	Anger

Building Trust - What does communication **with** trust look like and produce?

Trust is a cornerstone for relating and communicating more effectively with others.

With trust:

- Open and honest dialogue for effectiveness and improvement
- Increased performance
- Ideas and creativity flow freely
- Higher levels of mutual respect
- Higher morale
- People become engaged
- Productive with time
- People take personal responsibility

ACCEPT ➔ APPRECIATE ➔ CELEBRATE

Attitudes that Create or Reflect a Great Environment

Excitement	Influence
Energy	Commitment
Can-Do Attitude	Confidence
Peak Performance	Positive Energy
Team Effort	High Morale
"I'm Responsible" Mindset	Co-operative mindset
Ownership	Productivity
Personal Accountability	Peaceful Environment

The Dominant D Type's
Guide to Better Relationships and Communication

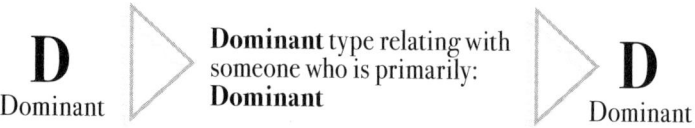

D Dominant — **Dominant** type relating with someone who is primarily: **Dominant** — **D** Dominant

Strengths:
Your mutual goals, admiration and the desire to get results can be very positive and affirming.

Struggles:
Power struggles are the most challenging. Neither of you wants to back down, give up or compromise.

Strategies:
Don't force issues. Allow this person to have some choices, control and authority. Don't argue or give ultimatums. Be direct and stick to business.

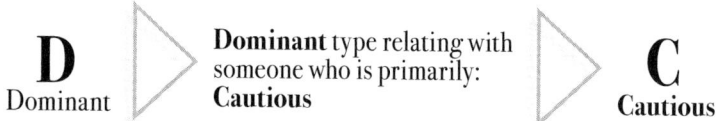

D Dominant — **Dominant** type relating with someone who is primarily: **Cautious** — **C** Cautious

Strengths:
Both of you focus on tasks and enjoy working independently. With this person's attention to detail, you can accomplish a lot together.

Struggles:
You tend to move quickly, whereas this person likes to think things through. Your focus is to get things done now, and his or her focus is to get things done right. Your desire to control things may discourage a cautious person, because this person does not like to feel pressured.

Strategies:
Do not rush or push this person. Do not criticize a cautious person. Be patient, and give him or her time to make decisions. Be willing to answer this person's questions and provide information in a polite manner. Do not expect this person to be a risk-taker like you.

Strengths, Struggles and Strategies of Your Relationship

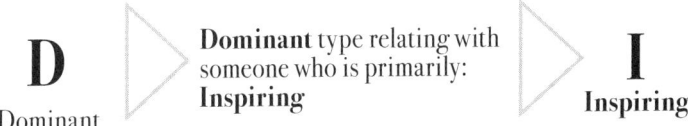

D Dominant — Dominant type relating with someone who is primarily: **Inspiring** — **I** Inspiring

Strengths:
Both of you are fast paced. This person may desire to please you and follow your leadership.

Struggles:
Your focus on getting things done can clash with this person's desire to have fun and "take-life-as-it-comes." This person does not share your drive to complete tasks. This person's focus is on people rather than on tasks.

Strategies:
Realize that this person does not usually focus on one thing, rather he or she focuses on many things. Help Inspiring (**I**) types finish tasks by working WITH them. Make things FUN! Allow them to talk and socialize.
Be positive and willing to express approval to them.
Be accepting of their expressions of emotion and feelings.

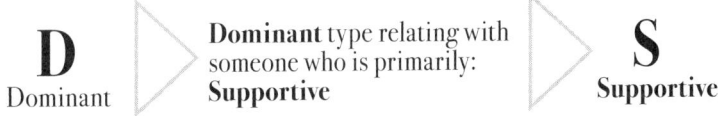

D Dominant — Dominant type relating with someone who is primarily: **Supportive** — **S** Supportive

Strengths:
You like to lead, and this personality type likes to follow and help. A supportive person will feel secure as long as you show controlled, stable behavior.

Struggles:
If you come on too strong, this person can feel intimidated and will take it personally. You may misunderstand this person's softhearted, easygoing nature as being "weak." Never confuse kindness for weakness. Remember that this person's focus is on people, and he or she tends to be slower paced.

Strategies:
Be patient and willing to spell things out, step-by-step when working on tasks. Communicate in a calmer, softer manner. Relax, and do not push. Express appreciation often. Be sincere.

The Inspiring I Type's
Guide to Better Relationships and Communication

I Inspiring — Inspiring type relating with someone who is primarily: **Dominant** — **D** Dominant

Strengths:
You both are outgoing and activity-driven. Both of you like to win. You may admire the strengths and achievements of this person.

Struggles:
You may find the other person to be too controlling, while you are too permissive. You are more social, while the other person is more task-driven.

Strategies:
Understand that a **D** type person is direct and results-oriented. Be more direct and get to the point with him or her. Do not be afraid of confrontation. Expect it, and do not take it personally. Work first, and THEN have fun.

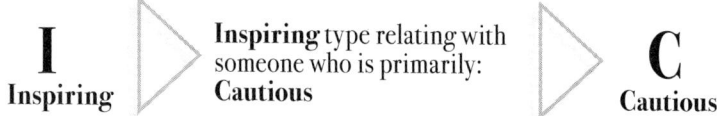

I Inspiring — Inspiring type relating with someone who is primarily: **Cautious** — **C** Cautious

Strengths:
Your opposite strengths provide a good balance to each other's weaknesses. You can learn from the other person's analytical nature, and this person can learn not to take things so seriously and to have more fun.

Struggles:
Your differences can lead to misunderstandings. You love to talk and be on the go, but the other person likes time alone. You are much more verbal, and it is easy for you to miss the other person's more indirect way of sharing concerns.

Strategies:
Tone down your emotional reactions. Be more factual and objective, especially in the face of conflict. Do not rush or push this person. Be specific in your communication, and expect this person to speak literally and to take things literally.

The Masterful Merchant

Strengths, Struggles and Strategies of Your Relationship

I Inspiring ▷ Inspiring type relating with someone who is primarily: **Inspiring** ▷ **I** Inspiring

Strengths:
Both of you live enthusiastically and enjoy being with people. You both like to have fun and tend to forgive easily.

Struggles:
Both of you tend to live emotionally and may compete for attention. You both are impulsive, and that can lead to challenges with following through with responsibilities and staying organized.

Strategies:
Remember to listen to the other person, because he or she likes to talk as much as you do. When working on important tasks, keep each other accountable, and be clear about who is responsible for what. Give sincere recognition of this person's abilities, ideas and contributions.

I Inspiring ▷ Inspiring type relating with someone who is primarily: **Supportive** ▷ **S** Supportive

Strengths:
Both of you are people-oriented. You like to talk and the other person likes to listen. You tend to get along very well.

Struggles:
Most struggles are related to pace. You like things fast-paced, exciting, spontaneous and with high energy. The other person likes things to be more calm, quiet and predictable.

Strategies:
Slow down your approach. Tone down your enthusiasm. Be sincere with praise and appreciation. Do not embarrass this person in public. Allow this person time to warm up and open up to you.

177

The Supportive S Type's
Guide to Better Relationships and Communication

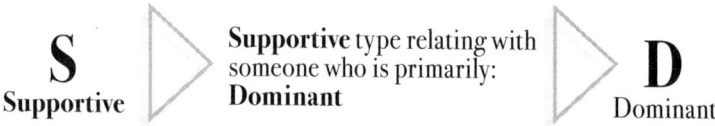

S Supportive → Supportive type relating with someone who is primarily: **Dominant** → **D** Dominant

Strengths:
You are a good supporter and encourager for this driven person who seeks to achieve and exert leadership.

Struggles:
This person can exhaust you by being controlling or by expecting instant action. You like to relax and go slow, but the other person does everything with a sense of urgency. You can become stressed, and this dominant person can become impatient.

Strategies:
Do not take it personally when this person takes action without you. Be more firm and results-oriented with this person. Be more direct, decisive and action-oriented when you deal with this person.

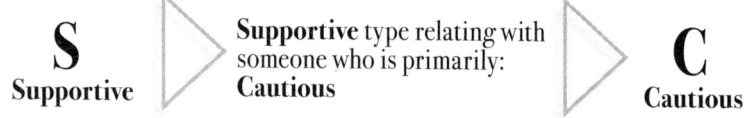

S Supportive → Supportive type relating with someone who is primarily: **Cautious** → **C** Cautious

Strengths:
Both of you are slower paced. Neither of you is pushy and you both prefer to avoid conflict. You can enjoy being together without a lot of conversation.

Struggles:
You tend to be sensitive while the other person has a tendency toward being critical. Your feelings-oriented nature can clash with the other person's logic-oriented nature. You want warm relationships, but the other person can seem more cold and impersonal to you.

Strategies:
Do not take this person's questioning, critical nature personally. This person likes to think deeply and analyze everything. Be willing to give in-depth answers. Do not push this person into closeness. Realize that this person is more Task-oriented than People-oriented, so he or she may not be as warm or sensitive as you are.

Strengths, Struggles and Strategies of Your Relationship

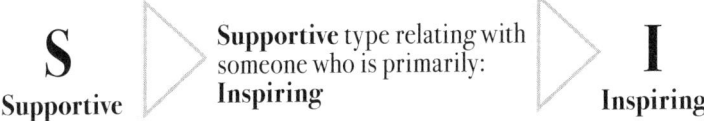

Strengths:
You tend to get along well, because you are both people-oriented. You both provide praise and appreciation to each other which you each need to feel good about yourselves.

Struggles:
Your biggest struggle will be keeping up with the pace of this person. This person likes excitement and activity, but you like things to be slower and calmer. Inspiring (I) type people have a large social circle, and that can seem overwhelming to you.

Strategies:
Be more outgoing and energetic with this person. An inspiring person is very impulsive. Be careful not to let this person talk you into something. Set some limits and do not feel pressured by this person's energy. Realize that he or she moves in large social circles, so do not take it personally if this person seems to give you fragmented attention.

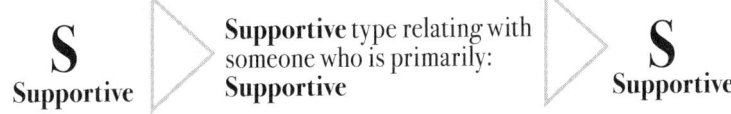

Strengths:
You have a lot in common and enjoy being with each other. Both of you like a relaxed, personal atmosphere.

Struggles:
The main struggle is in the area of communication. You both talk indirectly and do not insist on your own way. Neither of you likes to make hard decisions. Neither of you likes conflict or tension, so you avoid bringing up unpleasant issues.

Strategies:
Be willing to take more initiative and to be more decisive. Realize that some conflict and change is healthy. Draw out how the other person feels, and be willing to honestly share how you feel. Do not hide hurt feelings. Get issues and feelings out on the table and discuss them.

The Cautious C Type's
Guide to Better Relationships and Communication

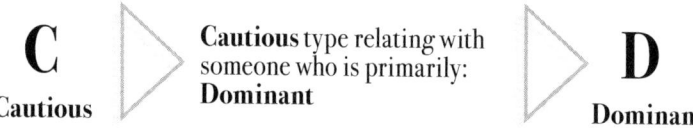

Strengths:
Both of you share a similar view toward accomplishing tasks. As long as you share the same goals, you can be very effective as a team.

Struggles:
You may have conflict if you take different approaches to accomplishing a task. You want things done "right," and this person is focused on getting things done quickly. They may think that you are over-analyzing things, while you may think that he or she is being too hasty.

Strategies:
Accept the fact that the **D**-type person needs to have some control and the ability πto take some action. Do not criticize or expect perfection. Instead, be willing to recognize and affirm this person's accomplishments.

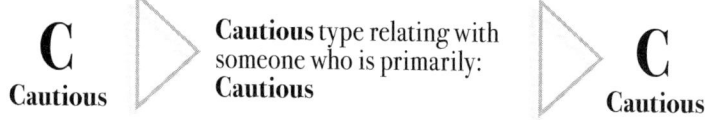

Strengths:
Both of you like to work hard on projects and focus on details and quality. You both tend to be serious and factual in your conversations.

Struggles:
There can be trouble when of you disagree on what is "right." Both of you can quickly shut down and withdraw. You both tend to wage a war of indirect communication.

Strategies:
Be open and flexible when this person suggests a different way of doing something. Be very careful with any criticism, because you know that criticism of your own work is one of your greatest fears. Do not set your standards so high that the other person feels he or she may not be able to reach them. Be specific with words of encouragement. Tell this person exactly what he or she did correctly and why you liked it.

Strengths, Struggles and Strategies of Your Relationship

C   Cautious   ▷ Cautious type relating with someone who is primarily: Inspiring ▷ **I** Inspiring

Strengths:
Your strengths balance each other out. You need the other person's freshness and fun, and the other person needs your discipline and logic.

Struggles:
Because you are opposites in personality, you may have a hard time understanding each other. You may not relate to this person's talkative, outgoing nature, and he or she may not relate to your analytical, cautious nature. Your standards may be too high for this person. You may naturally withhold the praise on which this person thrives.

Strategies:
You must modify your expectations of this person. Realize that this person will never have the attention to detail that you do. Look for this person's strengths, and be generous with recognition and approval. Listen enthusiastically to his or her stories. Most of all, do not push for perfection or this person may become discouraged and quit.

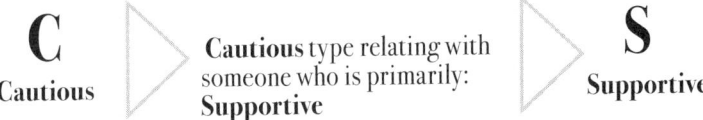

C   Cautious   ▷ Cautious type relating with someone who is primarily: Supportive ▷ **S** Supportive

Strengths:
Both of you like to take things slowly. You both enjoy a low-key relationship that is free from conflict.

Struggles:
You may become frustrated when this person does not appear to think things through the way you do or share your enthusiasm for key details. This person is feelings-oriented, so you may come across as cold and impersonal.

Strategies:
Be aware of your focus on doing tasks correctly. This person's focus is on peace and security in relationships. Be more warm and personal. Be careful not to criticize. Show sincere appreciation for any effort that is made. Do not set your standards too high, or this person may feel inadequate or simply give up.

Final thoughts...

A Masterful Merchant, like Pat O'Brien, knows the importance of creating a Customer First culture. Your A,B,C's (Attitude, Behavior and Concern,) for the customer's needs, not the needs of the Merchant, will be the secret to a business's longevity. Pat O'Brien had a method, the 7 **P**'s, that become his standard as well as his employees'. The success of his business depended on never compromising any of these principles. Do you have your own list of principles for operating your business? You may have the most innovative, useful, entertaining or delicious product with all the financial backing you could possibly need, but if you have not created a customer first culture, you will not be a Masterful Merchant. It is People who spend time and money wherever they please. And when they are pleased, they not only return, but are your best marketing tool!

We hope you have already begun using the DISC Model of Human Behavior. It is a fun and simple tool for unlocking a complicated and mysterious occurance...relationships! From a casual nod to balancing a check book with your mate, this understanding will make a healthy connection. And from employees loyalty to the company, to a loyal customer, this information will help you connect better by knowing the needs of different personality types. This is a simple concept. Like digging a hole is simple, just not easy, this information will take some time. Begin practicing with the people you currently work with or know!

There is one last important principle my years have taught me when it comes to connecting with people. Think about personally adopting this philosophy of business and life when it comes to working with other people... *I think I am right, but I may be wrong!* (Please see the next page for an explanation as well as further details.)

I think I am right, but I may be wrong!

Important principle: *I think I am right, but I may be wrong!* If you will admit the possibility that something could be wrong with yourself or with a particular situation, you will be able to correct it. But, if you refuse to admit the fact that something could possibly be wrong, you will not be able to see it, nor change it. When you admit something could be wrong, your mind and eyes alert and notify your Reticular Activating System to begin looking for other options, corrections, solutions or possibilities. There is a big difference between the statement, "Something could possibly be wrong here," versus the statement, "Everything is right." The secret to learning and growing in your own personality style is to recognize the fact that your strengths will carry you, but your weaknesses should concern you! By getting in touch with the possibility that there needs to be some attention and adjustment given to both strengths and weaknesses, you will double your effectiveness in becoming the successful person you were meant to be! We guarantee it!

Feel free to copy this page and cut it out along the dotted lines. It will become extremely helpful to you in the near future. Post it for a quick reference for that sales call, the upcoming interview, the teacher – parent conference, or if you just got pulled over for speeding! Remember, in order to be a Masterful Merchant you must connect with People by putting their personality needs first!

Quick Review

Understanding and meeting the needs of different personality styles is essential in building strong and healthy relationships.

D Type

Their Priority	Power
They Will	Decide quickly
In Order To	Solve Problems
Their Mindset	Get it done!

Needs:
- Choice
- Challenge
- Control

I Type

Their Priority	People
They Will	Actively engage
In Order To	Persuade others
Their Mindset	Fun & excitement

Needs:
- Approval
- Recognition
- Popularity

C Type

Their Priority	Procedure
They Will	Seek facts
In Order To	Uphold principles
Their Mindset	Obey the rules

Needs:
- Quality answers
- Excellence
- Value

S Type

Their Priority	Predictability
They Will	Seek routine
In Order To	Maintain status quo
Their Mindset	Let's get along

Needs:
- Appreciation
- Assurance
- Security

© Copyright— Personality Insights, Inc. All Rights Reserved www.personalityinsights.com

About the Author

Eric Demaree is the President of Carpet One Floor & Home, an international buying cooperative made up of over 1000 independently owned retail businesses. As a former Merchandising Vice President with the Home Depot and their Expo Design Centers, Eric has walked thousands of stores, gaining first-hand experience on how to help retailers and their people be more successful. A graduate of Lehigh University, Eric is a sought after speaker, community leader and a well-regarded professional in the field of retail merchandising and people development.